THE UNCOOK BOOK

NEW VEGETARIAN FOOD FOR LIFE

Juliano

with Erika Lenkert

ReganBooks

An Imprint of HarperCollinsPublishers

RAW THE UNCOOK BOOK

Juliano Brotman
with Erika Lenkert

HarperCollins books may be purchased for educational, business, or sales promotional use. For information please write: Special Markets Department, HarperCollins Publishers, Inc., 10 East 53rd Street, New York, NY 10022.

FIRST EDITION

Art Direction: P. R. Brown @ Bau-Da Design Lab, Inc.
Design: P. R. Brown and Diana Hong @ Bau-Da Design Lab, Inc.
Photography: Wynn Miller; Katherina Bosse, pp. 3 and 8
Food Styling: Victoria Granof

ISBN 0-06-039262-2
04 05 06 07 08 15 14 13 12 11

TABLE *of* CONTENTS

YOU COULD SAY I GREW UP IN LAS VEGAS,

Nevada, but more realistically my first fifteen years were spent in front of my television set. The concrete playgrounds of my neighborhood didn't exactly inspire me, so when I wasn't helping my father in his Italian restaurant, I stayed tuned as the networks recommended. At fifteen, I moved to Palm Springs, California, and that's when my life drastically changed from a spectator sport to a truly awesome interactive adventure. That move also sparked the genesis of Raw Cuisine, because in Palm Springs I began to understand that everything following nature's natural order lives in harmony with the planet and in complete health.

PREFACE

Prior to the move my only experiences with nature were through Sunday afternoon Tarzan specials. Suddenly, mountains, whose mighty peaks arched up into the clouds, were right outside my back door! My first day in town I ventured into the hills and found myself at the base of a cliff where trickling streams converged to form a rushing waterfall and glistening pool. An eagle soared out from the distant trees down to the pool and ascended with a fish clamped in her talons. Frogs sunbathed on giant rocks. And I, for the first time, felt a part of nature instead of a distant bystander watching the world on the tube. From that moment on, I felt a deep love and respect for nature.

One of the ways my adoration manifested itself was that I immediately became a vegetarian. The vegetarian route made sense in the natural world. Fruit possesses a seed to give birth to a new tree, which in turn gives us food, water, shelter, and oxygen: the essentials to human existence. Meanwhile, the physical results were another confirmation of my newfound beliefs. I started feeling lighter, more energetic, much less tired, and my body began to tone up, even though my workout regime didn't change. By 19 years of age I was totally vegan.

The next thing I discovered was certified organic foods. They cost a bit more, but their vibrant flavor was instantly priceless. After experiencing organic foods, I realized bland fruits and veggies are an unacceptable alternative, no matter how cheap they are.

As my excitement for this new lifestyle grew, so did my interest in raw fruits and vegetables. I was intrigued by leaves, roots, seeds, nuts, and herbs in their natural, uncooked state! I learned about the incredible nutritional content of plants and how sprouting seeds, grains, and beans actually manufactures vitamins naturally! I explored farmers' markets, talked to farmers, and discovered fascinating and unusual fruits and vegetables.

By the age of 22 I was inventing all types of new raw-food dishes with ingredients from every part of the world. My energy skyrocketed; I looked and felt better and thought more clearly and quickly than I ever had before! I was enjoying the most exquisite, unique, decadent food on the planet and my mentor was not some fancy cooking school, but the earth itself.

It was never my intention to open a restaurant. At 24 when I moved to San Francisco and hooked up with the San Francisco Raw Foods Group, the response to my cuisine was overwhelming. "You've got to open a restaurant!" became a daily mantra chanted by every single person who tasted my Raw creations. I borrowed $50,000 from my mom (her life savings), found a small commercial space near Golden Gate Park, and opened the doors to my restaurant with little more than a couple of dehydrators, blenders, a juicer, and a few bundles of organic groceries.

What came next was unprecedented, the kind of attention even deep-pocketed restaurants with a hefty public relations contracts wish they could obtain. The media, who like most people couldn't believe Raw food could taste this amazing, flocked to the place. Almost overnight my face and cuisine were plastered on the front page of *USA Today* and within the pages of *People* magazine, the *New York Times*, and *Vegetarian Times*. the *San Francisco Chronicle* hailed it the most innovative cuisine in the city. By its own merit Raw Cuisine shunned the stigma of "health food" and became recognized as a new, exciting style of food, which just happens to be great for you.

The national attention combined with the local public's reaction reaffirms my belief that as a culture we are not resigned to eating food that's bad for us. We are simply not prepared to give up flavor, convenience, and edible enjoyment for health. My Raw Cuisine continues to be received with astonishment and praise because it accomplishes what no other cooking style has in the past: the ultimate in flavor sensation, easy preparation, *and* optimum nutritional value.

That said, I want to clarify the purpose of this book. It is not to get you to shun your current lifestyle in exchange for a Raw meal consumed in the lotus position (although I bet you'd love it). It is rather to introduce you to (or reacquaint you with) the finest dining this planet has to offer; to give you the tools to understand your options and set out on a quest for the best in flavor; and to encourage you to question and reconsider the arguably suspicious processed foods we've been programmed to feed our bodies—the most vital instruments to our survival!

I'm not telling you how to live your life or offering guidelines or restrictions. The facts are the facts: I believe eating Raw is the healthiest and most harmonious way for us and the planet. However, I am offering you a wealth of suggestions so you can balance whatever lifestyle you choose with delicious, superior gourmet food that enriches your body, mind, and soul.

If you're in the neighborhood, you're always welcome for dinner. But wherever you are, make a point of experiencing life as it was meant to be: sensationally flavorful and totally RAW!

INTRODUCTION

WHAT IS RAW?

RAW IS CUISINE IN ITS REAL FORM: ORGANIC, FROM THE EARTH, AND UNCOOKED. FOR FOOD TO BE CONSIDERED RAW IT CAN BE CHOPPED, BLENDED, PUREED, JUICED, DEHYDRATED, OR COMBINED INTO INFINITE FLAVOR COMBINATIONS, BUT WHATEVER THE END RESULT, ALL RAW RECIPES ARE VEGAN (TOTALLY VEGETARIAN: NO MEAT, FISH, EGGS, OR DAIRY) AND "LIVING."

INGREDIENTS GROWN FROM THE EARTH ARE NATURAL AND AREN'T HARMFUL TO THE BODY; BASICALLY, THEY'RE ABOUT AS RAW AS YOU CAN GET. ANIMAL PRODUCTS, ON THE OTHER HAND, CARRY PARASITES AND BACTERIA AND ARE INJECTED WITH HORMONES, ANTIBIOTICS, AND STEROIDS. ORGANICALLY RAISED ANIMALS ARE OUT, TOO, BECAUSE THEY ARE JUST AS DIFFICULT FOR THE HUMAN BODY TO DIGEST AND DO NOT FALL UNDER THE SECOND REQUIRE-MENT, WHICH IS: RAW CUISINE IS ALSO "LIVING" FOOD. LIVING FOODS ARE FRUITS, VEGETABLES, GRAINS, BEANS, NUTS, ROOTS, AND SEEDS—VIRTUALLY EVERYTHING EDIBLE THAT GROWS FROM THE EARTH THAT HAS NOT BEEN COOKED. THIS IS THE MOST IMPORTANT ASPECT OF RAW CUISINE, BECAUSE FIRST OFF, IF YOU COOK FOOD IT'S NO LONGER RAW. MORE IMPORTANT, SCIENTISTS HAVE PROVEN THAT WHEN YOU SUBJECT ANY LIVING THING TO HEAT MUCH GREATER THAN 120 DEGREES, ITS NOURISHING ENZYMES DIE, WHICH MEANS THE MAJORITY OF ITS ESSENTIAL NUTRIENTS ARE DEAD, OR GREATLY DIMINISHED, WHEN YOU EAT THEM. THIS CONCEPT IS EASILY UNDERSTOOD BY LOOKING TO RAW SEEDS AS AN EXAMPLE; SEEDS MAY NOT LOOK LIKE THEY'RE "LIV-ING," BUT PLANT AND WATER THEM AND A FEW DAYS LATER THOSE LITTLE NUTRIENT STOREHOUSES HAVE SPROUTED TO LIFE AND ARE ON THEIR WAY TO BECOMING A PLANT. TRY THE SAME TEST WITH A ROASTED SEED AND, BELIEVE ME, THE RESULTS WILL BE FAR LESS EXCITING; A DEAD SEED SIMPLY CAN'T GROW.

CLEARLY PUT, RAW CUISINE FOLLOWS THE PRINCIPLE THAT FOR FOOD TO BE "RAW" AND "LIVING" AND THEREFORE THE MOST NUTRITIOUS AND IN THE FORM EVOLUTIONARILY INTENDED FOR HUMAN CONSUMPTION, IT MUST NEVER BE SUBJECTED TO HEAT ABOVE 120 DEGREES.

FINALLY, IDEALLY RAW CUISINE IS MADE FROM ORGANIC INGREDI-ENTS, WHICH ARE GROWN IN SOIL THAT IS ENHANCED WITH SUCH ORGANIC AIDS AS COMPOST, EARTHWORMS, NATURAL ROCK PROD-UCTS, OR BENEFICIAL BACTERIA. ORGANIC FARMING PRODUCES THE PUREST, MOST NUTRITIOUS FOOD BECAUSE IT DOESN'T USE PESTI-CIDES AND TOXINS, WHICH ARE EMPLOYED IN NON-ORGANIC FARMING. UNFORTUNATELY (AND IRONICALLY), NATURALLY GROWN PRODUCE IS NOT AS READILY AVAILABLE, OR AFFORDABLE, AS PESTICIDE-TREATED PRODUCE. NONETHELESS, IF YOU CAN ONLY GET YOUR HANDS ON THE STUFF FROM YOUR AVERAGE SUPERMARKET, WASH IT WELL AND EAT IT RAW, AND HEALTH-WISE YOU'RE STILL MILES AHEAD OF THOSE WHOSE BODIES ARE RUNNING ON COOKED FOODS.

WHY RAW?

WHY RAW? NOT BECAUSE IT GUARANTEES ME OPTIMUM HEALTH LIKE THE OTHER 80 MILLION SPECIES WHO EAT ONLY RAW. NOT BECAUSE IT'S THE LAST WORD IN NUTRITION. NOT FOR SAVING TIME OR MONEY, NOT FOR THE ENDLESS ENERGY IT PROVIDES ME, AND NOT BECAUSE IT HELPS THE PLANET BECAUSE INSTEAD OF DISCARDING PACKAGING, WHICH CREATES TRASH, I DISCARD SEEDS, WHICH GIVE LIFE. NO, NOT ANY OF THESE REASONS. SO WHY RAW? TASTE AND PLEASURE AND ONLY TASTE AND PLEASURE.

RAW FOOD HAS ULTIMATE PURE FLAVOR, MILLIONS OF TEXTURES, AND BEAUTIFUL EFFECTS ON BODY, MIND, SOUL, AND ENVIRONMENT! I'M NOT TALKING ABOUT 100 VARIATIONS OF SALAD. I'M TALKING ABOUT AN ULTRA-GOURMET CUISINE, WHICH FUSES ANCIENT AND MYSTICAL FOOD PREPARATION WITH A MODERN AND PRACTICAL LIFESTYLE. FROM SUN-BAKED PIZZAS, VEGAN SUSHI, THE BEST BURRITOS, AND WILD SPROUTED RICE DISHES, TO SANGRIA AND SHAKES, PUDDINGS AND PIES, ALL MY RAW RECIPES TASTE BETTER THAN THEIR COOKED, DEAD COUNTERPARTS.

BUT CULINARY SKEPTICS DON'T HAVE TO TAKE MY WORD FOR IT; EVEN MICHAEL BAUER, *SAN FRANCISCO CHRONICLE*'S HIGHLY REGARDED RESTAURANT CRITIC, REVIEWED MY RESTAURANT IN SAN FRANCISCO AND INFORMED HIS READERS, "IN A CITY KNOWN FOR INNOVATIVE COOKING, RAW LIVING FOODS BEATS THEM ALL. ANY TRUE GOURMAND SHOULD GO AT LEAST ONCE AND BE AMAZED AT THE VARIETY OF FLAVORS AND COMBINATIONS."

SO PLEASE, GET THE IDEA OF WILTED LETTUCE AND BLAND CARROTS OUT OF YOUR MIND! YOU'RE ABOUT TO ACQUAINT YOURSELF WITH THE VIBRANT FLAVORS AND MIRACULOUS NUTRITION OF PLANT LIFE IN A WAY YOU NEVER HAVE BEFORE. RAW!

DINNER AT MY HOUSE

IF YOU CAME OVER FOR DINNER (AS ALL PEOPLE I MEET DO, WHETHER THEY'RE INTO RAW FOOD OR NOT), IT'S LIKELY YOU'D EXPERIENCE A MEAL AS YOU NEVER HAVE BEFORE. WHETHER IT WAS SERVED IN SAN FRANCISCO, LAS VEGAS, OJAI, OR KATMANDU, PRIOR TO YOUR ARRIVAL I'D SET OUT FOR FOOD AND DO SOME "LOCAL HARVESTING." I SCOUR THE NEIGHBORHOOD FOR EDIBLE PLANT LIFE THAT MOST PEOPLE DON'T EVEN CONSIDER BEFORE THEY GO SPEND THEIR HARD-EARNED MONEY AT THE GROCERY STORE. I MIGHT COME BACK WITH FRESH-PICKED LEMONS, AVOCADOS, OR PERSIMMONS FROM THE HOLLYWOOD HILLS. IN SAN FRANCISCO IT COULD BE THE PRESIDIO'S FINEST WILD MUSHROOMS OR LETTUCES. IN OJAI IT'D BE MULBERRIES, ORANGES, OR OLIVES.

NEXT I'D SET MY TABLE, WHICH IS USUALLY THE FLOOR, WITH PILLOWS, INDONESIAN TEXTILES, BOWLS AND BEESWAX CANDLES, GLASS CHINESE SOUP SPOONS (THE ONLY GLASS SILVERWARE THERE IS!), AND FLOWERS PICKED FROM THE NEIGHBORHOOD. YOU WILL NOT FIND NAPKINS, BUT RATHER FINGER BOWLS FILLED WITH FILTERED WATER AND A SLICE OF LEMON.

YOUR INITIAL REACTION TO THE EVENING MIGHT BE SIMILAR TO ONE FOOD CRITIC'S, WHO LATER CONFESSED SHE WAS SKEPTICAL WHEN I THREW TOGETHER OUR DINNER OF FAT MUSHROOM SOUP, THAI GREEN PAPAYA SALAD, AND PASTA MARINARA WITH NOTHING MORE THAN A KNIFE AND A BLENDER. APPARENTLY SHE WORRIED SHE WOULDN'T BE SATED AND WOULD HAVE TO PIT STOP FOR FAST FOOD ON THE WAY HOME. SHE ALSO WONDERED WHETHER BRINGING A BOTTLE OF WINE WAS OFFENSIVE TO ME. ("HEY, IT'S VEGAN AND RAW, IT'S COOL!" I TOLD HER.)

WHEN WE SAT DOWN TO EAT AND NAPKINS WERE NOTICEABLY ABSENT, SHE SEEMED HORRIFIED. WHEN THE BURRITOS' JUICY CONTENTS TRICKLED ONTO MY HANDS AND I LICKED IT OFF, SHE STARED INCREDULOUSLY AND ATE WITH THE UTMOST CONCERN FOR GETTING FOOD ANYWHERE BUT IN HER MOUTH. BUT BY THE END OF THE EVENING SHE CONFIDED IN ME THAT SHE REALIZED THERE WAS SOMETHING SERIOUSLY DEMENTED WITH THE FACT THAT EATING NATU-RALLY, WITHOUT ALL THE EXPECTED POMP AND CIRCUMSTANCE, IS A FRIGHT-ENINGLY FOREIGN EXPERIENCE. SHE ALSO ADMITTED THAT SHE WAS NOT ONLY ENTIRELY SATISFIED, BUT ALSO FELT ELATED, COMFORTABLY ENERGIZED, SATISFIED, AND EXCITED TO COME OVER AGAIN. SHE'S NOW A REGULAR AT MY DINNER PARTIES AND IS NO LONGER AFRAID OF GETTING FOOD ON HER HANDS.

1

LEARNING TO UN-COOK

Most people unfamiliar with Raw cuisine are immediately intimidated; the idea of eating only what nature has provided us, absurd as it is, has become a foreign concept. The recipes and their ingredients can seem extensive and mysterious. But the truth is, preparing raw meals is remarkably simple and takes less time than cooking.

Much of the prep work can be done in bulk and in advance, so the ingredients will be ready to use at mealtimes. A recipe, for example, may call for sprouted buckwheat, which is a recipe in itself. Sprout extra and keep it in the refrigerator and you're a step ahead next time.

RAW AND SIMPLE

I know the long ingredients lists can appear daunting and that many dishes call for a dozen chopped or minced ingredients. Usually they are ultimately thrown into a blender or food processor and the only reason I require they are chopped at all is so that you will use the correct amount. Once you become familiar with approximating the measurements, you can throw many of the ingredients into the blender whole, which will save you enormous amounts of time. Even if a recipe does call for a substantial amount of mincing and chopping, there are ways to make that easier on yourself. (see "Using Your Knives" later in this chapter.) Regardless, prep time for Raw cuisine takes about the same amount of energy as preparing any other gourmet dish and you'll ultimately save time because you'll never have to watch over something in the oven or on the stove.

Don't let the Kitchen Equipment list (later in this chapter) intimidate you either; you can almost always work around the utensils you don't have. If your kitchen lacks a dehydrator, for example, you can use an oven (see "Dehydrator" definition in this chapter.) If you don't have a food processor you can usually get away with using a blender. Haven't invested in a juicer? Just pick up your fresh-pressed juice or pulp at an organic grocery store or juice bar.

So don't look at the text and think it's too much work; a little chopping and mincing here, blending and dehydrating there, and before you know it, you'll be Raw and loving it.

ABOUT
THE INGREDIENTS

I always say, "The supermarket is full of food, but there's nothing to eat" because the corner store rarely carries raw, living, and organic ingredients. The best place to buy the ingredients required in this book, as well as everything you put into your body, is at any organic supermarket. If you are unfamiliar with any ingredient, the folks at the health food store will be able to help you find it, and I've also included a glossary at the back of this book, which includes a description of uncommon ingredients. The organic supermarket is also where you can pick up vegetable pulps or fresh squeezed juices if you don't have a juicer at home.

INGREDIENTS

As long as your idea of cooking isn't tossing a frozen dinner into the microwave, you probably have most of the equipment needed to prepare Raw cuisine. If you don't, they'd be great additions to your kitchen.

KITCHEN EQUIPMENT

Blender   Useful for everything from smoothies to soups, sauces, and puddings, the blender is the most commonly used instrument in preparing Raw cuisine. If you don't have a food processor, you can almost always substitute a blender, though if you're blending a lot of dry, thick ingredients you'll often have to scrape the sides of the blender with a rubber scrapper to help turn the ingredients over.

Blender Jar   Any small mason jar can screw onto your blender base! Using a blender jar is great for blending small quantities and is probably already somewhere in your kitchen.

Food Processor   So handy in the kitchen, it can chop, blend, mix, mince, and shred; it's not essential but makes Raw preparation a lot easier and works with dry ingredients when a blender can't.

Dehydrator   The Raw chef's version of the oven, I use a dehydrator to do all my "baking."

Cookies, chips, crusts, candy, breads, meat loaf, superior dried fruits, and more are all prepared in a dehydrator, which blows hot air, but never gets hot enough to burn you or your food. Best of all, a dehydrator can avoid subjecting food to heat hotter than 120°F, which allows all the delicate nutrients that are usually burned out of cooked foods to remain intact.

If you're not committed enough to buy a dehydrator (yet), you can use an oven, but only if you set it at the lowest possible temperature (usually around 150°F) and make sure the oven is no hotter than 100°F. If using the oven you should use Pyrex cookware.

Dehydrator Sheets   These sheets, which usually come with a dehydrator, are in solid and mesh variations (netted plastic), as well as special food-grade plastic sheets.

The Green Power Juicer   This special juicer not only makes good juices, but it shreds, grinds, creams, and

homogenizes! And all this for under $400.00! There are a variety of juicers on the market, but Green Power Juicers are the best.

Coffee Grinder   This common kitchen item is ideal for making flour from nuts and for grinding tough spices. I don't use a coffee grinder often in this book, but when I do, it's very useful (especially when it comes to grinding sun-dried lime).

Using Your Knives   If I didn't know how to use my knives, I would be so insane from chopping all day I probably wouldn't be a Raw fooder. The best way to get though a big chopping job is to stack-chop, which means you basically divide and conquer. If I'm dicing a tomato, I don't slice off one piece, dice it, and continue with the next piece. I slice all the pieces, stack them, on top of each other and dice the whole pile at once. If you don't do it already, get in the habit of stack-chopping and food preparation will be a breeze.

ABOUT SOAKING & SPROUTING

Simply stated, seeds, grains, and beans are a storehouse for nutrients that will nourish the plant as it grows and matures. "Sprouting" is germination, a process where all the vitamins, minerals, proteins, and essential fatty acids dormant in raw seeds, grains, and beans activate and multiply. The only way to induce sprouting is to soak the seeds, grains, or beans you're trying to sprout in water, then give them time to grow. (Of course, the seeds, grains, and beans must be living, or raw, in order for growth to occur.) Sprouting also eliminates certain acids and toxins in plant life that would otherwise interfere with digestion. Sprouted beans, for example, are easier to digest than un-sprouted beans because in the process their protein content increases and their starch content decreases.

"Soaking" is similar to sprouting in that you allow the ingredients to bathe in water. However, the goal in soaking something, such as nuts or dates, which do not sprout, is to change their consistency. I blend soaked nuts when I want them to have a creamy texture; un-soaked nuts tend to blend into a more oily and granular texture. Dates also become creamier after a good soaking.

How to Sprout

Place seeds, beans, or grains into a large bucket or bowl and cover with filtered water. Let them soak for the amount of time determined in the "Sprouting & Soaking Table" (see page 9). Once soaked, place a colander over the bucket or bowl and drain all the water. Leave the seeds, beans, or grains in the colander overnight. Rinse the seeds, beans, or grains the next day in a bucket or bowl filled with water and briefly swirl them around with your hand.

Return them to the colander until the next rinsing, 1 day later. Rinse once daily until your grains, seeds, or beans sprout a "tail" about $1/4$ inch long. (For information on approximate sprouting times, see the Sprouting & Soaking Table on page 9.) Once the sprouted food's tails are long enough, place the sprouts in a container in the refrigerator; this helps to slow the growing process and preserve the sprouts. The longer the tail grows, the more water it retains; sprouts with longer tails have less flavor and tend to be watery. Sprouts keep for 3 days in the refrigerator.

SPROUTING

ow To Soak

How to Soak

When soaking nuts, they should be placed in water for the time determined in the "Sprouting & Soaking Table." Almonds, for example, should be soaked for 8 hours, unless the recipe says otherwise. Soaked and drained nuts keep in the refrigerator for 3 days. Other ingredients I soak include dates and sunflower seeds.

Sprouting & Soaking Table

	SOAKING TIME HOURS	SPROUTING TIME DAYS
Almonds	8	No sprouting
Barley	6	2
Buckwheat	6	2
Chickpeas (a.k.a.: Garbanzo Beans)	8	2–3
Flax Seeds	$1/_2$	No sprouting
Kamut	7	2–3
Lentil Beans	7	3
Oat Groats	6	2
Quinoa	2	1
Rye	8	3
Sesame Seeds	6	2
Spelt	7	2
Walnuts	4	No sprouting
Wheat berries	7	2–3
Wild rice	9	3–5
All other nuts	6	No sprouting

ABOUT JUICING & PULP

Aside from easily juiced fruits such as orange or lemon, there is no way to juice or produce pulp from a fruit or vegetable in your kitchen if you don't have a juicer. If you do have one, you simply press the raw fruit or vegetable through the machine; the juice comes out one end and the pulp is what's left. If you don't have one and a recipe calls for fresh squeezed beet juice or carrot pulp, for example, you can always get it from an organic juice bar (at most health food stores).

If you don't have all the ingredients required in a recipe, don't worry about it. I swap ingredients all the time; whenever I don't have maple syrup I use honey. When I don't have enough honey I add some dates. With a combination of ingredients the result is more complex and wonderfully sweet than the maple syrup alone. Experiment and become comfortable with the ingredients.

GETTING STARTED

Start with a few easy recipes. A few of my favorites are Pasta Marinara, Fetuccini Alfredo, and any of the burritos. When you realize how simple uncooking is, move on to sprouting, and making Living Buckwheat Crust.

When preparing Raw cuisine the two **spices** that really matter are: 1) Salt, for the incredible way it brings out the flavor of food, and 2) Jalapeño, which when used correctly takes a dish to a whole other level and drives the palate wild! Jalapeño fulfills an additional necessity in Raw cuisine; it adds *heat.*

These peppers give the illusion of **raising the temperature** of a dish that may not be necessarily even spicy. In small portions it's still present, lurking in the background and enhancing the tongue's roller coaster ride of flavors and textures. The difference between good food and amazing food is pushing these two ingredients—salt and jalapeño—to their limit; to the point where you've *almost,* but not quite, added too much. Instead, it tastes perfect!

One essential element for human survival is water. So what have we evolved into doing? We cook the water out of our food and then we drink dirty tap water to make up for it.

Say you've tried a few recipes and have come to the obvious realization that Raw Cuisine is not only easy, but it tastes best and results in feeling better than you ever have before. The next step is to head to the health food store and stock up on a few essential ingredients, which will allow you endless combinations of Raw Cuisine bliss. All of the following ingredients, with the exception of fresh produce, last indefinitely. Buy all these and your kitchen will be well stocked and raw-ing to go.

1 bottle extra virgin olive oil
1 jar ground cumin
1 jar ground curry
1 jar ground cinnamon
1 bottle Nama Shoyu
1 bag Celtic sea salt
2 pounds raw kamut, spelt, or wheat berries
2 pounds raw buckwheat
2 pounds raw chickpeas
3 onions
5 heads fresh garlic
$1/4$ pound fresh ginger
4 jalapeño chilis
7 lemons
10 oranges
$1/2$ pound pistashios
1 package golden miso
1 bottle raw honey
1 jar tahini
$1/2$ pound raw walnuts
$1/2$ pound raw sunflower seeds
1 bottle marinated sun-dried tomatoes
5 to 20 Nori sheets
2 bunches cilantro
1 bunch parsley
1 head of red leaf or romaine lettuce
2 bunches basil
$1/4$ pound mushrooms
3 pounds tomatoes
3 ripe avocados
5 non-ripe avocados
1 bottle black miso
$1/2$ pound dates
1 pound raw carob

2

SOUPS

BUTTERNUT S

BUTTERNUT SQUASH SOUP

FOR SOUP:

3 cups butternut squash, peeled, seeded,
 and chopped
1 mango, cubed
2 teaspoons curry
4 cups orange juice
$1/2$ cup honey or dates

FOR GARNISH:

1 plantain or banana, sliced
$1/2$ cup chopped mint
A pinch of minced jalapeño
1 mango, seeded, peeled, and diced

In a blender, combine the butternut squash, mango,
curry, orange juice, and honey or dates and blend
until creamy. Garnish with plantain or banana slices,
mint, jalapeño, and mango.
Serve immediately after blending.

$^1/_3$ cup black or brown sprouted rice
(for recipe see page 7)
4 cups Rejuvelac (for recipe see page 194),
coconut water, seaweed water, vegetable broth,
filtered water, or fresh-squeezed orange juice
$^1/_3$ cup carrots, julienne
$^1/_3$ cup chopped broccoli
$^1/_3$ cup chopped red bell pepper
$^1/_3$ cup sprouted beans
$^1/_3$ cup chopped purple cabbage
$^1/_4$ cup Nama Shoyu or 1 $^1/_2$ teaspoons Celtic sea salt
$^1/_4$ cup red wine
$^1/_4$ cup chopped shallots
$^1/_3$ cup diced portobello mushrooms
$^1/_4$ cup black miso
1 teaspoon minced jalapeño
4 $^1/_2$ teaspoons minced garlic
1 tablespoon minced ginger
$^1/_3$ cup green beans
$^1/_3$ cup chopped tomato
$^1/_3$ cup olive oil
$^1/_4$ cup fresh-squeezed lemon juice
$^1/_3$ cup diced onion
2 tablespoons rosemary, de-stemmed and chopped
$^1/_3$ cup fresh parsley, chopped
2 tablespoons fresh oregano, chopped
$^1/_3$ cup fresh basil, chopped
$^1/_3$ cup fresh cilantro, chopped
$^1/_2$ teaspoon dulse or ground kelp

Serves 4

THIS SOUP IS HEARTY ENOUGH THAT IT CAN EASILY BE A MAIN COURSE.

SUN STEW

Combine the rice and all the above ingredients in a gallon-size jar. Cover the jar, shake it well, leave it in the hot sun for 1 hour and serve. Refrigerate leftovers.

THIS IS A THIN LIGHT SOUP THAT'S MADE HEARTY BY ADDING CHOPPED SAVORY FRUITS.

Serves 2

1 cucumber, peeled
1 cucumber, unpeeled
$1/3$ cup fresh herbs (sage, rosemary, oregano, thyme, tarragon and basil)
$1/3$ cup fresh cilantro, chopped
$1/3$ cup fresh mint, chopped
$1/3$ cup fresh parsley, chopped
$1/4$ cup garlic, with peel
1 tablespoon ginger, with peel
$1 1/2$ teaspoons jalapeño
$1/4$ cup Nama Shoyu or 2 teaspoons Celtic sea salt
$1/3$ cup olive oil
$1 1/2$ cups fresh-squeezed lemon juice
4 cups fresh-squeezed orange juice
4 avocados, peeled and seeded
4 whole tomatillos, remove papery husks

EXTRA AVO SOUP

To make this soup hearty, chop up the unpeeled cucumber, 1 tomatillo, 1 avocado, and anything else you have on hand and divide evenly among two soup bowls. In a blender combine the peeled cucumber, fresh herbs, cilantro, mint, parsley, garlic, ginger, jalapeño, Nama Shoyu or Celtic sea salt, olive oil, lemon juice, orange juice, 3 avocados, and 3 tomatillos and blend well. Pour blender contents into chunky-fruit-filled soup bowls and serve immediately.

Serves **2**

NRG Soup

THIS SOUP IS EASY TO MAKE AND SO DELICIOUS!

Even if you don't like your food spicy, try adding small amounts of hot peppers—not enough to cause any degree of heat to the dish, just enough for a little interesting background flavor.

1 full recipe of Water (for recipe see page 224)
1 cup diced tomato
1 cup chopped mint
$\frac{1}{2}$ cup chopped onion
$\frac{1}{2}$ cup chopped red bell pepper
$\frac{1}{2}$ cup corn, cut from the cob
1 tablespoon minced garlic
$\frac{1}{2}$ tablespoon minced ginger
$\frac{1}{2}$ tablespoon habanero chili
$\frac{1}{3}$ cup Nama Shoyu or 1 $\frac{1}{2}$ teaspoons Celtic sea salt
1 medium apple, chopped
2 cups fresh-squeezed orange juice

Blend all ingredients and serve immediately.

Serves 2

3 medium beets (for 1 cup of beet juice)
1 pound carrots (for 1 cup fresh carrot juice)
$1/4$ cup chopped green onion
$1/2$ cup green cabbage, shredded
1 teaspoon dill
$1/2$ cup beet, finely grated
1 large avocado, spooned out into chucks
$1/2$ apple, thinly sliced

RAW BORSCHT

THIS VIBRANT SOUP WILL BLOW BABUSHKA'S MIND!

Put beets and carrots through a juicer so that you have a cup of juice from each. (You can also buy fresh juice at any health food store.) Place beet juice, carrot juice, green onion, cabbage, and dill into blender and blend. In a serving bowl mix grated beet, avocado, and the blender contents. Chill the borscht in the refrigerator until you're ready to serve it. Garnish the borscht with apple slices and serve.

HEARTY
LENTIL SOUP

Serves 2

1 cup Almond Milk (see recipe on page 250)
  or filtered water
2 tablespoons minced onion
$1/4$ cup diced red bell pepper
$1/2$ cup avocado
$1/2$ cup chopped tomato
1 teaspoon minced garlic
2 tablespoons fresh dill, minced
2 tablespoons Nama Shoyu
  or 1 teaspoon Celtic sea salt
1 teaspoon minced jalapeño
1 cup sprouted lentils
  (for recipe see page 7)
  dash of paprika

Put all ingredients *except the lentils* into a blender or food processor and puree well. Add the lentil sprouts and blend or process for 1 or 2 seconds, 3 times. Pour into serving bowls, garnish with paprika, and eat immediately.

ENTIL SOUP

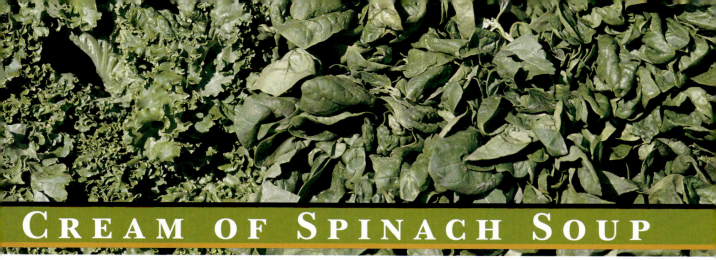

CREAM OF SPINACH SOUP

Serves 4

IT PUTS POPEYE'S CANNED STRENGTHENER TO SHAME.

2 cups fresh squeezed tomato, carrot,
  and/or vegetable juice
2 cups chopped spinach
2 tablespoons chopped escarole, optional
$1/2$ medium-size avocado
2 tablespoons minced garlic
1 teaspoon minced jalapeño
1 teaspoon minced ginger
2 tablespoons chopped green onions
$1/4$ cup Nama Shoyu
  or 1 $1/2$ teaspoons Celtic sea salt
1 tablespoon fresh-squeezed lime juice
1 tablespoon fresh mint leaves, chopped
$1/3$ cup fresh cilantro, chopped
$1/2$ cup olive oil
$1/8$ cup white wine
$1/4$ cup chopped shallots
$1/2$ cup portobello mushrooms, thinly sliced

In a blender or food processor, blend the juice,
spinach, and escarole, optional. Add the remaining
ingredients and blend or pulse-chop very briefly. Chill
and serve garnished with thinly sliced mushrooms.

3 medium beets or 1 cup beet juice
1 tablespoon minced jalapeño
2 tablespoons minced garlic
1 tablespoon minced ginger
5 cups fresh-squeezed orange juice
$1/4$ cup chopped green onion
1 cup grated cabbage
1 teaspoon fresh chopped dill
2 or 3 avocados, cubed
$1/2$ cup of your favorite fresh herbs
$1/2$ cup grated carrots
$2/3$ cup olive oil
$1/2$ cup fresh-squeezed lemon juice
$1/2$ apple, cut into thin slices
1 teaspoon Celtic sea salt

RED, RAD, AND RUSSIAN!

Serves 4

RAW BORSCHT #2

If you have a juicer, juice the beets into 1 cup of beet juice. Pulp can be used in another recipe within 10 hours if kept refrigerated. If you don't have a juicer, buy fresh beet juice from a health food store. In a mixing bowl combine the beet juice with all the ingredients except the apple slices. Shake and serve immediately garnished with thin apple slices.

ORSCHT #2

$^1/_2$ cup walnuts
    filtered water for soaking walnuts
1 $^1/_2$ tablespoons white miso
$^1/_2$ cup zucchini, shaved with
    a vegetable peeler into long strips
$^1/_2$ cup diced tomato
1 tablespoon minced garlic
1 tablespoon fresh dill, minced
1 tablespoon fresh parsley, minced
1 tablespoon chopped green onion
1 teaspoon minced jalapeño
1 ear of corn cut from the cob
1 cup filtered water
$^1/_3$ cup olive oil
2 tablespoons Nama Shoyu
    or 2 teaspoons Celtic sea salt

Serves 2

SOUP

CORNY SOUP

Soak walnuts for 4 to 8 hours and drain. Set aside. In a food processor, combine white miso, zucchini, tomato, garlic, dill, parsley, green onion, and jalapeño and puree for about 8 seconds. Add corn and process for about 8 more seconds. Pour soup into serving bowls. Just before you're ready to eat, combine in a blender the walnuts, water, olive oil, and Nama Shoyu or Celtic sea salt and blend until liquefied, about 3 minutes. Add blender contents to soup bowls equally.

MAKE THIS GREAT SOUP ON A HOT SUMMER EVENING USING THE TENDER, SWEET, WHITE IN-SEASON CORN!

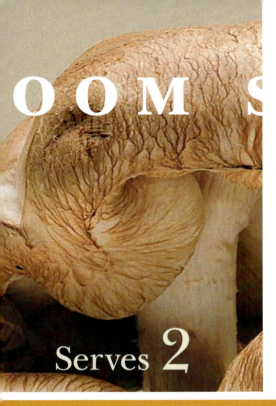

O O M S

Serves 2

FOR SOUP:

$1/4$ cup fresh cilantro, chopped and moderately packed
1 tablespoon fresh basil leaves, chopped
1 tablespoon fresh fennel, de-stemmed and chopped
2 tablespoons fresh dill, de-stemmed and chopped
$1/2$ teaspoon pineapple sage leaves, chopped
$1/2$ teaspoon fresh lemon thyme, de-stemmed chopped
$1/2$ teaspoon fresh oregano leaves, chopped
1 teaspoon fresh parsley, chopped
$3/4$ cup tomato (preferably orange cherry tomatoes)
$1/4$ cup olive oil
3 tablespoons Nama Shoyu or 2 teaspoons Celtic sea salt
$1/4$ cup Rejuvelac, coconut water, seaweed water, vegetable
   broth, filtered water or fresh-squeezed orange juice
$1/2$ teaspoon fresh squeezed lemon juice, optional
$1/2$ teaspoon minced ginger, optional
$1/2$ teaspoon minced garlic, optional

FAT MUSHROOM SOUP

FOR GARNISH:

$1/2$ cup fresh portobello mushrooms, diced
1 tablespoon fresh dill, de-stemmed and chopped
1 teaspoon Mellowkraut (for recipe see page 241)
2 teaspoons red bell pepper, chopped
1 teaspoon of your favorite edible flower petals

Place all soup ingredients in blender and blend for 30 to 45 seconds, until just smooth (you should still be able to see pieces of the herbs and tomato). Pour into serving bowls and float garnishes on top in following order: portobella, dill, Mellowkraut, bell pepper, flower petals. (Be sure to add the portobello first; it's buoyant and acts as a raft for the other garnishes.) Eat the soup immediately after blending.

$^1/_2$ cup sliced plantains

$^1/_2$ cup diced apple

$^1/_2$ cup diced avocado

$^1/_2$ cup pitted dates, diced

$^1/_2$ cup diced kiwi

$^1/_2$ cup diced strawberries

$^1/_2$ cup diced pineapple, optional

$^1/_2$ cup pomegranate seeds
   (if it's autumn and they're in season)

$^1/_2$ cup berries of your choice, diced

1 teaspoon minced jalapeño
   (optional; omit if you're making
   this dish for children)

2 cups fresh-squeezed orange juice

$^2/_3$ cup fresh-squeezed lemon juice

1 cup dates, whole

1 $^1/_4$ cups frozen strawberries or other berry

NEW MOON FRUIT STEW

THIS IS A FRUITARIAN DISH, WHICH MEANS IT'S MADE FROM NOTHING BUT FRUIT. ALONG WITH THE INGREDIENTS LISTED, YOU CAN CUSTOMIZE THIS RECIPE WITH ANY OTHER SWEET FRUITS OF YOUR CHOICE.

In a serving bowl combine plantain, apple, avocado, dates, kiwi, strawberry, pineapple, pomegranate seeds, other berries, and $^1/_2$ teaspoon jalapeño, optional. Set aside. In a blender combine orange juice, lemon juice, dates, frozen strawberries or other berries, and the remaining $^1/_2$ teaspoon of jalapeño, optional, and blend until frozen fruit is blended and sauce has a creamy consistency. Pour blender contents over bowl of fruit and serve immediately.

Serves 4

$1/2$ cup diced cucumber

$1/2$ cup diced apple

$1/2$ cup diced avocado

$1/2$ cup sliced yellow or zucchini squash

$1/2$ cup diced kiwi

$1/2$ cup frozen strawberries, sliced

$1/2$ cup other berries, diced

$1/2$ cup diced pineapple

$1/2$ cup pomegranate seeds

$1/2$ cup chopped red bell pepper

$1/4$ cup black sprouted rice
 (for recipe see page 7)

1 teaspoon minced jalapeño, optional

2 cups fresh-squeezed orange juice

$2/3$ cup fresh-squeezed lemon juice

$2/3$ cup dates

1 $1/4$ cups frozen strawberries or other berries

2 tablespoons olive oil

SPICY FRUIT SOUP
A SAVORY VARIATION ON THE NEW MOON FRUIT STEW.

Serves 4

In a serving bowl combine cucumber, apple, avocado, squash, kiwi, strawberries, other berries, pineapple, pomegranate seeds, red bell pepper, rice, and $1/2$ teaspoon jalapeño. Set aside. In a blender combine orange juice, lemon juice, dates, strawberries, or other berry, $1/2$ teaspoon jalapeño, optional, and olive oil and blend until frozen fruit is pureed and sauce has acquired a creamy consistency. Pour blender contents over bowl of fruit and serve immediately.

RUIT SOUP

FOR SOUP:

1 ½ cups fresh carrot juice
1 tablespoon mint leaves
1 teaspoon minced jalapeño
1 teaspoon minced ginger
2 teaspoons minced garlic
⅓ cup avocado
2 teaspoons olive oil
2 tablespoons Nama Shoyu
or 1 ½ teaspoons Celtic sea salt
1 tablespoon basil leaves

FOR GARNISH:

2 tablespoons avocado, diced
2 teaspoons fresh mint leaves, chopped
2 teaspoons diced red bell peppers
2 teaspoons scallions, chopped

Serves 2

FIERY LAVA

LAVA

Blend soup ingredients for 30 to 45 seconds, until creamy. Divide soup into serving bowls and garnish with avocado, mint, bell peppers, and scallions. Eat immediately.

WHEN ONE SKEPTICAL DINER ENJOYED LUNCH AT RAW AND SAID, "I could really get into this raw foods thing except for the fact that I love hot soup on cold, winter evenings." I said, "Fiery Lava will have you pouring sweat and racing to open a window! Any other questions?"

10 cherry tomatoes, halved
2 teaspoons minced garlic
2 teaspoons minced ginger
$2/3$ cup fresh mint, chopped
$2/3$ cup fresh basil, chopped
$2/3$ cup fresh cilantro, chopped
1 tablespoon chopped walnuts
$2/3$ cup Marinated Portobellos (see recipe on page 238)
2 tablespoons chives and/or green onions, chopped
3 tablespoons fresh squeezed lime juice
$1/2$ teaspoon fresh Thai chili, minced
1 tablespoon minced galanga
a few strips of red bell pepper
1 cup fresh coconut meat, chopped
1 medium-size avocado
2 tablespoons lime leaves (kaffir lime), well minced
1 tablespoon lemon grass, well minced
4 cups coconut water (from 2 to 3 coconuts)
$2/3$ cup Nama Shoyu
$2/3$ cup olive oil
1 tablespoon Curry Chutney (for recipe see page 228)

Serves 4

Tom Khai

In a serving bowl combine cherry tomatoes, garlic, ginger, mint, basil, cilantro, walnuts, mushrooms, chives and/or green onions, lime juice, Thai chili minced, galanga, and red bell pepper. Stir and set aside. Grind the lime leaves (kaffir lime) in a coffee grinder or mince by hand. Set aside. If you have a Champion, mill about 1 cup of coconut meat and put it in a blender. If you don't have a Champion, chop 1 cup of coconut meat by hand and put it in the blender. Just before you're ready to eat, add to the blender the galanga, avocado, lemon grass, coconut water, Nama Shoyu, olive oil, remaining Thai chili, and Curry Chutney. Blend until the soup is creamy with no remaining chunks. Pour blender contents over ingredients in the serving bowl, mix, and serve right away.

$2/3$ cup red bell pepper, julienne
1 tablespoon minced ginger
1 tablespoon minced garlic
$1/2$ teaspoon fresh Thai chili, minced
$2/3$ cup cherry tomatoes, halved
$2/3$ cup portobello mushrooms, chopped
$2/3$ cup fresh mint, chopped
$2/3$ cup fresh basil, chopped
$2/3$ cup fresh cilantro, chopped
1 tablespoon galanga, minced
$1/2$ cup Nama Shoyu
2 tablespoons minced lime leaves (kaffir lime)
1 tablespoon lemon grass, well minced
1 cucumber, peeled
$2/3$ cup olive oil
$1/2$ cup fresh-squeezed lemon juice
3 tablespoons cashew butter
1 tablespoon Curry Chutney
  (for recipe see page 228)
3 cups coconut water (from 1 to 2 coconuts),
  seaweed water, or filtered water

Serves 4

PASSION SOUP

In a serving bowl combine red bell pepper, ginger, garlic, Thai chili, cherry tomatoes, mushrooms, mint, basil, cilantro, galanga, and Nama Shoyu. Put the lime leaves in a coffee grinder and grind them well (mincing by hand works, too). Transfer the lime leaves to a blender and add the lemon grass, cucumber, olive oil, lemon juice, cashew butter, Curry Chutney, and liquid (coconut water is preferred but you can also use seaweed water or filtered water). Blend until creamy and pour over ingredients in the serving bowl. Serve immediately.

Serves 2
FENNEL SOUP

FOR SOUP:

2 cups fennel bulb, chopped
1 cucumber, peeled
10 celery stalks, chopped
$2/3$ cup fresh cilantro, chopped
$1/2$ cup chopped cucumber, unpeeled
1 medium red, purple,
  or orange bell pepper, chopped

FOR GARNISH, OPTIONAL:

$1/2$ cup Cottage Cheese
  (for recipe see page 258)
$1/2$ cup avocado, diced

In a blender blend peeled cucumber, fennel bulb, and celery (if you have a juicer, use it instead). Add $1/4$ cup filtered water if blender is having a hard time "turning over." Pour into serving bowls and top with cilantro, chopped cucumber, and bell pepper. Garnish with a dollop of my amazing Cottage Cheese or avocado and serve.

3

SALADS

HERE'S WHAT I MAKE MY SALAD OUT OF AT MY RESTAURANT.
You can make your salads with any or all of these delicious ingredients. They're easy to find at farmers markets and specialty stores.

ANCIENT MIX

anise hyssop
arugula
borage
bronze fennel
chickweed
endive
frisee
meadow rue
mint
mizuna
red oakleaf
salad burnet
society garlic
summer purslane
curly cress

Serves 4

Combine $1/2$ cup of each green in a salad bowl, add your favorite dressing, toss, and serve.

TRADITIONAL ITALIAN SALAD

Serves 4

2 cups diced tomatoes
1 cup fresh basil, chopped
$^{1}/_{2}$ cup olive oil
1 cup Maui onion, chopped
1 tablespoon fresh oregano
$^{1}/_{3}$ cup lemon juice
1 $^{1}/_{2}$ teaspoons Celtic sea salt
1 tablespoon black olives, chopped
1 cup cubed avocado

Combine ingredients in a large bowl.
Mix and serve.

RICOTT

FOR SALAD:

2 cups chopped fennel bulbs

2 tablespoons fresh lemon thyme, chopped

2 tablespoons fresh creeping thyme, chopped

2 tablespoons fresh silver thyme, chopped

2 tablespoons fresh sage, chopped

2 tablespoons fresh rosemary,
   de-stemmed and chopped

2 tablespoons salad burnet

2 tablespoons fresh Greek oregano

2 tablespoons chocolate mint

$1/2$ cup red bell pepper, chopped

ENSALATA A LA RICOTTA Y FINOCCHIO

FOR DRESSING:

$1/4$ cup white wine

1 cup coconut water (from 1 coconut),
   seaweed water, orange juice, or filtered water

$1/2$ cup Raw Ricotta Cheese
   (for recipe see page 255)
   or Mac Cream
   (for recipe see page 254)

3 tablespoons balsamic vinegar
   (if aged 150 years or longer use
   triple the amount listed)

$1/4$ cup fresh-squeezed lemon juice

$1/4$ cup olive oil

Serves 4

In a salad bowl combine fennel bulbs, lemon thyme, creeping thyme, silver thyme, sage, rosemary, salad burnet, Greek oregano, chocolate mint, and bell pepper. In a blender combine white wine, selected water/juice, Raw Ricotta Cheese, balsamic vinegar, lemon juice, and olive oil. Blend well and pour blender contents over salad mix. Toss and serve.

COLE SLAW

Serves 2

2 cups purple cabbage, shredded
1 large unpeeled cucumber, diced
1 large shredded carrot
$1/4$ cup shredded onion
1 $1/2$ tablespoons cumin seeds
1 $1/2$ teaspoons ground cumin
3 $1/2$ tablespoons fresh-squeezed lemon juice
$1/2$ cup diced tomato
3 tablespoons Nama Shoyu
   or 1 teaspoon Celtic sea salt
$1/3$ cup olive oil
1 tablespoon minced garlic

Combine the above ingredients in a serving bowl. Mix and serve.

LAW

Serves 2

2 cups shredded cabbage
$1/_4$ cup shredded onion
1 cup shredded carrot
1 recipe of Mayo #2

Combine the above ingredients
in a serving bowl. Mix and serve.

CREAMY COLE SLAW

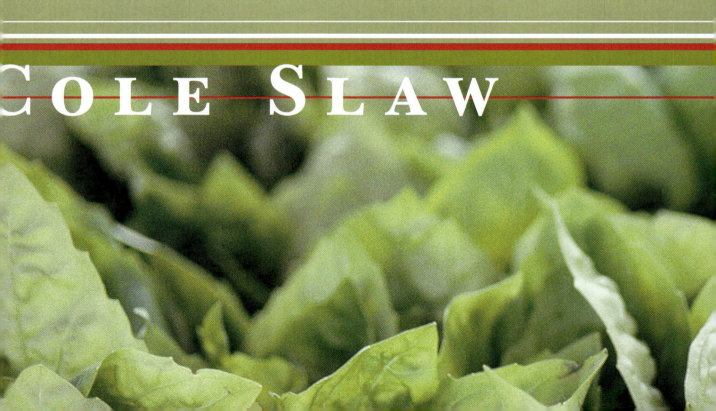

COLE SLAW

1 head of red leaf, butter, or romaine lettuce
1 cup fresh oregano, de-stemmed and chopped
$1/2$ cup fresh thyme, de-stemmed and chopped
$1/2$ cup fresh rosemary, de-stemmed and chopped
$1/2$ cup fresh sage, de-stemmed and chopped
$1/2$ cup fresh cilantro, chopped
$1/2$ cup fresh parsley, chopped
$1/2$ cup fresh basil, de-stemmed and chopped
1 cup fresh mint, de-stemmed and chopped
3 cups RAW Restaurant's House Dressing
 (for recipe see page 212)

Serves 2

Combine the lettuce and "weeds" in a salad bowl and drown in Raw Restaurant House Dressing.

DROWNING WEED SALAD

¹/₂ cup green papaya, shredded on the side
   of the grater with larger holes
2 cups ripe papaya, diced
2 avocados, cubed
1 cup shredded carrot on the
   side of the grater with larger holes
2 tablespoons lime leaves (kaffir lime), finely minced
1 tablespoon lemon grass, finely minced
¹/₂ cup diced red bell pepper
¹/₄ cup chopped scallion
¹/₄ cup chopped red onion
¹/₄ cup chopped shallots
¹/₂ cup sliced cucumber, unpeeled
¹/₂ cup fresh cilantro, chopped
1 cup fresh mint, chopped
¹/₂ cup fresh basil, chopped
1 tablespoon Curry Chutney (for recipe see page 228)
²/₃ tablespoon minced galanga
1 tablespoon minced garlic
¹/₂ tablespoon minced ginger
1 teaspoon Thai chili, minced
²/₃ cup olive oil
¹/₄ cup Nama Shoyu
¹/₄ cup fresh-squeezed lime juice
¹/₄ cup fresh-squeezed orange juice

Mix & munch!

Serves 2

THAI GREEN PAPAYA SALAD

Serves **2**

NANO'S SALAD

$1/4$ cup pomegranate seeds

$1/4$ cup olive oil

$1/4$ cup fresh-squeezed lemon juice

1 cup any type of lettuces, mixed

$1/2$ cup white, yellow, or red onion, chopped

1 teaspoon Celtic sea salt

1 cup avocado, cut into big chucks

$2/3$ cup cherry tomatoes, halved

2 tablespoons Buckwheaties
   (for recipe see page 231)

2 sheets of nori

Combine everything but the nori
in a salad bowl. Serve with nori
(the bread) on the side.

VERYTHING SAL

EVERYTHING SALAD

Anything in your refrigerator that needs to
get eaten. Chop, grate, and dice your
 fridge combo. Serve with your favorite
RAW dressings, which are listed in
Chapter 11.

BREADS

LIVIN

LIVING BUCKWHEAT
PIZZA CRUST

1 ½ cups sprouted buckwheat groats
  (for recipe see page 7)
¼ cup olive oil
Garlic spices and herbs to taste
⅔ cup carrot pulp
⅔ cup soaked flax seeds

Makes 1 10-inch crust

B u

Once you're comfortable

with this recipe you can experiment with your own variations to make any number of wonderful breads. I've added minced sun-dried tomatoes, and/or minced fresh garlic, and/or minced green onion or chives to the dough and formed bread sticks and twists.

Put the groats in a mixing bowl, dribble the olive oil (I also dribble a *little* date syrup) over them, add carrot pulp and flax seeds. (If using a blender, add a little liquid and use a rubber scraper to help turn over.) Mix with a large spoon. Then scoop the groats, in batches, into a food processor or blender. Coat a solid plastic dehydrator sheet or a cookie sheet with oil and scoop 3 or 4 big scoops of dough onto it (a mound about 6 inches in diameter). If the dough is sticky, use filtered water or fresh squeezed orange juice to moisten your hands and the dough's surface; it will be easier to work with. With moistened hands, shape the dough into a rough square or circle and pat top of crust flat. Smooth the top and edges to form a 10″ × 10″ square. Check depth at center by inserting the tip of a knife. It should be the same depth as your edges, $^1/_4$ to $^1/_2$ of an inch deep. Dehydrate at 99°F for 7 or 8 hours, until the crust is dry enough to transfer. Lift the crust with a spatula and transfer to mesh dehydrating rack for faster double-sided dehydrating. Dehydrate for another 7 or 8 hours. When done, your crusts should be very dry, without a hint of moistness or softness. These can be kept 1 month (if the bread is very dry), loosely wrapped or covered and stored in a dry place.

$^1/_3$ cup chopped red bell pepper
$^1/_3$ cup fresh cilantro, chopped
$^2/_3$ cup sun-dried tomatoes
1 $^1/_4$ cups diced tomatoes
1 teaspoon minced jalapeño
1 tablespoon minced garlic
1 tablespoon olive oil
$^1/_4$ cup Nama Shoyu
   or 1 teaspoon Celtic sea salt
2 cups flax seeds

Makes **12** 4-inch crackers

FLAX SEED CRACKERS

Place bell pepper, cilantro, sun-dried tomato, tomatoes, jalapeño, garlic, olive oil, and Nama Shoyu or Celtic sea salt into food processor (or blender) and puree. Transfer contents into a large bowl and mix in the flax seeds. Spread flax seed mixture onto oiled solid dehydrator sheet. Dehydrate at 90°F for 4 hours (or when top is dry), cut them into desired shapes (I make 3×3 inch squares) and transfer them onto a mesh dehydrating rack. Dehydrate until crackers are crisp, about 5 hours.

$^1/_4$ **cup almonds**
$^1/_4$ **cup walnuts**
3 pitted dates
water for soaking nuts and dates
2 cups sprouted wheat berries, kamut, or spelt (for recipe see page 7)
$^1/_4$ **cup shredded apple**
1 teaspoon minced garlic
1 teaspoon fresh parsley, minced
1 tablespoon olive oil

ESSENE BREAD #1

Makes 1 loaf

Soak almonds and walnuts in water for at least 2 hours. In a separate container, soak dates in water for 1 hour. Drain nuts and dates and toss them into a food processor along with the rest of the ingredients and puree into a dough. (If you have a Champion juicer, after pureeing, run it through.) On a solid dehydrating sheet form dough into a loaf about 1 $^1/_2$ inches tall, 3 $^1/_2$ inches wide, and 6 inches long. Dehydrate at 90°F for 13 to 17 hours. When done, the loaf should be crisp on the outside and moist on the inside.

SENE BREAD

A SWEETER VERSION OF #1.

$^1/_4$ cup almonds
$^1/_4$ cup walnuts
2 cups sprouted kamut, spelt,
  or wheat berries
  (for recipe see page 7)
$^1/_2$ cup chopped apple
3 pitted dates
$^1/_4$ cup olive oil

ESSENE BREAD #2

Soak the almonds and nuts in water for at least 2 hours. In a separate container, soak the dates in water for 1 hour. Drain the nuts and dates, combine them in a food processor with the remaining ingredients, and puree. (If you have a Champion juicer, after pureeing, run it through.) On solid dehydrator sheets, form the pureed dough into a loaf about 1 $^1/_2$ inches tall, 3 $^1/_2$ inches wide and 6 inches long. Dehydrate at 90°F for 13 to 17 hours. When done, the loaf should be crisp on the outside and moist on the inside.

Makes 1 loaf

BAGELS & LOX

$1/2$ cup freshly scraped coconut
  meat from a young coconut
1 pound carrots
1 teaspoon seaweed
  or ground seaweed
4 slices Pumpernickel Rye Essene Bread (for recipe, see
  page 60)
2 slices onion
2 slices tomato
$1/2$ avocado, sliced into wedges

Serves 2

In a juicer, juice the carrots to make $2/3$ cup fresh carrot juice (or buy the juice from a health food store). Combine the juice with coconut meat and seaweed; marinate until the coconut meat is a rich orange color. This is your lox. Place lox on a piece of Pumpernickel Rye Essene Bread or any of the other Essene breads. Add onion, tomato, and avocado (the cream cheese). Shalom!

THEY DON'T JUST
TASTE LIKE
BAGELS & LOX;
THEY TASTE LIKE
THE BEST BAGELS
& LOX ON THE
PLANET!

BUCKWHEATIES CEREAL

LIVING CEREAL, NOT DEAD STUFF IN A BOX.

1 cup Buckwheaties (for recipe see page 231)
$1/3$ cup dates
1 cup sliced berries or other fruit
2 cups Nut Milk (for recipe see page 250)
$1/2$ cup sliced bananas or plantains

Combine the above ingredients in a cereal bowl.

Mix and serve.

Serves 1

BERRY PORRIDGE

Serves 1

2 cups oat groats
water for soaking groats
1 cup dates
$1/2$ cup berries

Soak oak groats in enough water to cover for at least $1/2$ hour. Drain groats and place in a blender with dates and berries. Blend and serve.

Makes 1 flat loaf

TRY NOT TO EAT IT ALL BEFORE USING SOME IN THE BAGEL & LOX RECIPE!

Make way more than one batch at once; the bread keeps for a very long time.

2 cups sprouted rye
(for recipe see page 7)
1 $\frac{1}{2}$ tablespoons minced garlic
$\frac{1}{4}$ cup olive oil
$\frac{1}{3}$ cup raw carob powder
1 tablespoon caraway seeds
1 $\frac{1}{2}$ teaspoons Celtic sea salt

Combine ingredients in a food processor and puree. On solid dehydrator sheets, form the pureed dough into a loaf about 1 $\frac{1}{2}$ inches tall, 3 $\frac{1}{2}$ inches wide and 6 inches long. Dehydrate the loaf at 90°F for 13 to 17 hours. When done, the loaf should be crisp on the outside and moist on the inside.

PUMPERNICKEL
RYE ESSENE BREAD

Makes 16 pieces of Real Toast

THIS TAKES ABOUT 40 MINUTES
(plus dehydrating time) to make, but is so worth it!
I recommend quadrupling the recipe so you'll have lots on hand.

$^1/_2$ cup sprouted black-eyed peas (optional; for recipe see page 7)

2 $^1/_2$ cups sprouted kamut, spelt or wheat berries (for recipe see page 7)

1 $^1/_2$ cups fresh-squeezed orange juice

1 teaspoon Celtic sea salt

1 cup fresh herbs of choice, chopped fine

1 teaspoon paprika

$^1/_2$ tablespoon cayenne

$^1/_2$ teaspoon jalapeño

$^1/_2$ cup chopped onion

$^1/_4$ cup chopped garlic

1 cup flax seeds

In a food processor combine black-eyed peas (optional), 2 cups sprouted grains, orange juice, Celtic sea salt, herbs, paprika, cayenne, jalapeño, onion, and garlic and process into dough. Mix in (by hand) flax seeds and remaining $^1/_2$ cup sprouted grains. Form dough into 8 × 8-inch square crusts, making sure crusts are no more than $^1/_4$ inch thick. Dehydrate for 8 to 10 hours or until toasty. Quarter each 8 inch crust to render 4 × 4-inch toast slices. Store in a cool, dry place. Real Toast keeps for a month.

REAL TOAST

Makes 1 loaf

2 cups sprouted kamut, spelt, or wheat berries (for recipe see page 7)

$1/2$ cup chopped apples

$1/2$ mango, peeled and seeded

2 large dates, pitted

$1/3$ cup fresh-squeezed orange juice

2 tablespoons olive oil

$1/4$ cup maple syrup or honey

2 tablespoons mango, cubed

2 tablespoons apples or other fruit, diced

In a food processor, puree the sprouted grains, chopped apples, mango, dates, orange juice, olive oil, maple syrup or honey. (If you have a Champion, after puree-ing, run it through.) Transfer the mixture to a bowl and stir in the cubed mango and diced apples.

On a solid dehydrator sheet, form the pureed dough into a loaf about 1 $1/2$ inches tall, 3 $1/2$ inches wide and 6 inches long. Dehydrate in a dehydrator at 90°F for 13 to 17 hours. When you take the loaf out of the dehydrator, it should be crisp on the outside and moist on the inside.

MANGO ESSENE BREAD

THIS IS SAUDI ARABIAN SWEET BREAD.
Get exotic and throw in a pinch of curry.
And definitely make more than one batch!

1 cup walnuts and/or almonds
1 cup flax seeds
1 jícama, sliced thin
1 $1/2$ teaspoons Celtic sea salt
$1/2$ cup olive oil
$1/4$ cup red bell pepper, diced
$1/2$ cup minced garlic
$1/2$ cup lemon juice

Slice jícima as thin as possible. Spread one layer of jícima on a solid dehydrator sheet. Powder flax seeds, walnuts and/or almonds and combine with salt, olive oil, red bell pepper, lemon juice, and garlic in a bowl and mix thoroughly. Drizzle mixture over jícima. Dehydrate in a dehydrator at 100°F for 8 hours or until chewy.

GARLIC BREAD

YOU'LL BE CURSING ME if you spend 8 hours dehydrating eight little patties, so double, triple, or quadruple the recipe and be happy, mon!

Makes 8 falafel patties

1 1/2 cups sprouted chickpeas
  (garbanzo beans, for recipe see
  page 7)
1 cup sprouted sunflower seeds
  (for recipe see page 7)
1 tablespoon minced garlic
2 cups fresh cilantro, chopped
1/2 cup tahini
1/4 cup Nama Shoyu or 1 tablespoon Celtic sea salt
2 tablespoons fresh parsley
1/2 cup chopped onion
1/2 cup fresh-squeezed lemon juice
1/2 cup olive oil
1 1/2 teaspoons Curry Chutney
  (for recipe see page 228)
1 1/2 teaspoons cumin
2 teaspoons sun-dried lime

FALAFEL PATTIES

Combine all ingredients in a blender and blend well. Form blended mixture into 1-inch by 3-inch elongated patties, place them on an oiled mesh dehydrator sheet, and dehydrate for 8 hours at 90°F. When the falafel patties are done they have a nice crust on the outside and are moist on the inside.

5

WHEN MY FRIEND ORDERED A MUSHROOM SANDWICH AT A CHIC LOS ANGELES RESTAURANT, I HAD TO ADMIT IT LOOKED AND SMELLED GREAT. SO I MADE MY VERSION OF THE SANDWICH AND LET MY SAME FRIEND PUT IT TO THE TASTE TEST.

GUESS WHO WON!

Serves 1

PORTOBELLO SANDWICH

1 recipe Marinated Portobello (for recipe see page 238)
2 slices of Real Toast (for recipe see page 61)
a few lettuce leaves
1 slice of tomato
2 thin slices red bell pepper
Mayo (for recipe see page 245)

Prepare 1 recipe Marinated Portobello. Dehydrate the marinated mushroom on a dehydrator sheet for 1 to 2 hours at 100°F. Place mushroom between two slices of Real Toast. Add your favorite green leaf, tomato, red bell pepper, and Mayo.

B L T

B L T

IT DOESN'T TASTE ANYTHING LIKE ONE; IT'S BETTER LOOKING AND TASTING.

2 slices Real Toast (for recipe see page 61)
1 tablespoon Mayo #2 or Raw House Dressing
 (for recipes see pages 245 and 212)
$1/_4$ cup chopped spinach
1 tomato slice
1 onion slice
2 tablespoons fresh cilantro, chopped
1 tablespoon fresh-squeezed lemon juice
1 tablespoon olive oil
1 tablespoon Nama Shoyu or $1/_4$ teaspoon Celtic sea salt
$1/_2$ teaspoon curry

Serves 1

Between two slices of Real Toast place Mayo #2 or Raw House Dressing, spinach, tomato, onion, cilantro, lemon juice, olive oil, Nama Shoyu or Celtic sea salt, and curry. Serve.

1 cup sunflower seeds (sprouted or un-sprouted)
1 cup almonds or walnuts
water for soaking the nuts and seeds
$1/8$ cup fresh-squeezed lemon juice
$1/2$ teaspoon garlic
$1/2$ teaspoon powdered dulse
$1/8$ cup Nama Shoyu or 1 $1/2$ teaspoons Celtic sea salt
$1/4$ cup chopped onion
$1/4$ cup chopped celery
$1/4$ cup fresh parsley, chopped
$1/2$ teaspoon powdered kelp
$1/2$ teaspoon minced garlic
8 pieces Real Toast (for recipe see page 61)
4 tomato slices
8 romaine lettuce leaves

NO ONE WILL EVER KNOW!

Makes 4 sandwiches

TUNA SANDWICH

If you're using sprouted sunflower seeds you do not need to soak them, but if you're using un-sprouted seeds, they will need to soak for at least 2 hours. (For information on how to sprout, see "How to Sprout" on page 7.) Soak the nuts in a container filled with water for at least 1 hour.

In a food processor, blend the sunflower seeds, nuts, lemon juice, garlic, dulse, Nama Shoyu or Celtic sea salt until smooth. Transfer the food processor contents to a mixing bowl and fold in the onion, celery, parsley, powdered kelp, and garlic. Spread the mixture between two pieces of Real Toast with the tomato and romaine lettuce leaves.

NUT BUTTER AND JELLY SANDWICHES

$^1/_4$ cup nut butter (almond or cashew, and, of course, raw)
$^1/_4$ cup mashed berries
2 pieces of Real Toast (for recipe see page 61)

Serves 1

Spread nut butter and mashed berries between the slices of Real Toast.

FAST SANDWICH

Serves 1

$^1/_2$ avocado, sliced

2 pieces of Real Toast (for recipe see page 61)

Squash avocado between two pieces of Real Toast.

AST SANDWICH

RAW CH

RAW CHIPS

4 cups sliced sweet potato, sunchokes, carrots, zucchini and/or anything else that crunches cut into the shape of chips.

Munch.

BANANA CHIPS

MAKE A LOT OF THESE; THEY'RE ADDICT
4 bananas

Serves 2   Cut bananas in $1/4$ inch disks and dehydrate
until crispy, around 8 hours.

BANANA FINGERS

4 bananas

Cut bananas lengthwise into $1/2$ inch strips and dehydrate until chewy, around 8 hours.

Serves 2

ALMOND BUTTER BANANA

Serves 1

1 banana
$1/3$ cup raw almond butter or cashew butter
Black Tar, to taste (optional; for recipe see page 183)

Slice a banana in half lengthwise. Spoon on raw almond or cashew butter and drizzle with Black Tar!

SWIRLED BUBBLE GUM

CHEW ON DAY-GLO, SWEET, ZINGING BUBBLE GUM ALL DAY— AND YOU CAN EVEN SWALLOW!

1 pint strawberries
2 kiwis
1 mango

Slice the mango, strawberries and kiwis $^1/_4$ inch thick, lay them on a mesh dehydrator rack, and dehydrate them at 90°F for around 8 hours or until they're sticky and chewy. To test if they're done, curl and swirl the fruit between your palms; if they hold their shape when rolled up, they're ready. Share!

5 sunchokes, beets, carrots, or yams
1 recipe of Nacho Cheese (for recipe see page 259)
1 $1/2$ cups Guacamole (for recipe see page 88)
1 cup fresh cilantro, chopped
1 cup Raw Salsa (for recipe see page 232)
  or Cilantro Salsa (for recipe see page 233)
1 cup Sour Cream #2 (for recipe see page 265)
1 cup sprouted lentil or black beans
  (for recipe see page 7)
1 cup Marinated Portobello (for recipe see page 238)
1 teaspoon minced jalapeño
Celtic sea salt or Nama Shoyu to taste

Serves 4

MACHO NACHOS

Slice sunchokes, beets, carrots, or yams into thin, chip-like slices. Arrange them on a platter and top them with Nacho Cheese slices, Guacamole, cilantro, Raw Salsa or Cilantro Salsa, Sour Cream #2, beans, and Marinated Portobello. Sprinkle with jalapeño, salt or Nama Shoyu and serve.

ACHOS

NATED CAVIAR

Serves 4 as an appetizer

FOR MARINADE:

1 tablespoon apple cider vinegar

1 tablespoon Umeboshi plum paste (optional)

1 tablespoon Nama Shoyu

1 tablespoon fresh-squeezed lemon juice

$1/_4$ cup fresh-squeezed orange juice

FOR CAVIAR:

2 cups blackberries, blueberries, raspberries, pomegranates, or papaya seeds (papaya seeds are best when marinated overnight)

1 lemon

MARINATED CAVIAR

In a mixing bowl whisk together apple cider vinegar, Umiboshi plum paste, Nama Shoyu, lemon juice, and orange juice. Pour the marinade over the selected caviar. Spoon the marinated caviar into goblets, forming rounded portions. Drizzle with lemon and serve.

Serving suggestions: Present the caviar with a side of decoratively arranged RAW Chips (see page 75 for recipe) and/or Real Toast (see recipe on page 61). Any RAW cheese also pairs well with caviar.

4 cups chopped rutabagas (for "brown rice")
and/or turnips (for "white rice")
and/or beets (for "red rice")
and/or yams (for "orange rice")

SECOND RICE

Serves 4

Place root vegetable of choice in a food processor and process until it has a granular rice-like consistency.

MASHED POTATOES

3 cups chopped cauliflower
1 cup cashews
$\frac{1}{2}$ cup fresh-squeezed lemon juice
$\frac{1}{2}$ cup fresh thyme, chopped
1 tablespoon minced garlic
1 tablespoon Celtic seasoning

Blend cauliflower in a blender using a little lemon juice and add remaining ingredients. If you have a Green Power juicer, use it instead. Hocus pocus! You have mashed potatoes!

IDEALLY SERVED SMOTHERED IN GRAVY (FOR RECIPE SEE PAGE 223).

1 cup red bell pepper, chopped
1 cup sliced carrots
$\frac{1}{2}$ cup chopped green onions
$\frac{1}{2}$ cup red beets, julienne
$\frac{1}{4}$ cup purple cabbage, sliced thin
$\frac{1}{2}$ cup peas
$\frac{1}{2}$ cup yam, julienne
1 cup water chestnuts, peeled and chopped
1 cup sprouted brown rice (for recipe see page 7)
$\frac{1}{2}$ cup sprouted wheat berries (optional; for recipe see
    page 7)
1 tablespoon minced ginger
1 tablespoon minced garlic
1 teaspoon minced jalapeño
$\frac{1}{4}$ cup Nama Shoyu
$\frac{1}{4}$ cup fresh-squeezed lemon juice
$\frac{1}{2}$ cup olive oil
2 teaspoons orange rind, grated

FRIED RICE

Combine the above ingredients, except orange rind, in a serving
bowl. Mix, sprinkle the rind on top and serve.

Serves 2

LEAVE THE AVOCADO PITS IN THE GUACAMOLE. IT'LL KEEP THE GUACAMOLE GREEN.

Makes around 3 cups

2 cups avocado
$1/4$ cup olive oil
$1/4$ cup chopped green onions
$1/2$ cup fresh cilantro, chopped
1 teaspoon minced jalapeño
$1/2$ cup chopped tomato
1 $1/2$ teaspoons Celtic sea salt
$1/4$ cup fresh-squeezed lime juice

In a mixing bowl mash avocado and olive oil with a wooden spoon, and in rapid, circular strokes, whip until fluffy. Fold in green onions, cilantro, jalapeño, tomato, Celtic sea salt, and lime juice.

GUACAMOLE

UACAMOLE

THEY GO DOWN BEST WITH A CHEESE BURGER, COLE SLAW, KETCHUP, AND A MILK SHAKE.

Serves 4

2 avocados, peeled and cut into wedges
1 recipe Nacho Cheese (for recipe see page 259)

Wrap flexible sections of Nacho Cheese around skinned avocado wedges. Devour!

FRENCH FRIES

ENERGY GUACAMOLE

2 cups avocado
$1/3$ cup olive oil
$1/4$ cup green onions, chopped
$1/2$ cup fresh cilantro, chopped
1 teaspoon minced jalapeño
1 teaspoon minced ginger
1 tablespoon minced garlic
$1/2$ cup red cherry tomatoes, diced
1 $1/2$ teaspoons Celtic sea salt
$1/4$ cup fresh-squeezed lime juice
1 $1/2$ teaspoons Juliano's Spice Chutney (for recipe see page 227)
1 teaspoon Mexican Spice Chutney (for recipe see page 227)
$2/3$ cup sprouted beans of your choice
  (for recipe see page 7)
5 medium-size sunchokes, sliced into $1/4$-inch chips
2 carrots, cut into long, thin strips
1 teaspoon pomegranate seeds
a sprinkling of your favorite edible flowers

In a mixing bowl combine the avocado and olive oil and with masher, mash with a rapid circular stroke until fluffy. Fold in the green onions, cilantro, jalapeño, ginger, garlic, tomato, Nama Shoyu or Celtic sea salt, lime juice, Juliano's Spice Chutney, Mexican Spice Chutney, and sprouted beans. Form the guacamole into a mound in the center of a serving dish. Surround it with sunchoke chips. For a sunny look, place carrot strips between the chips. Sprinkle with pomegranate and flower petals. Serve.

ENERGY GUA

MANITOK WILD

I CALL IT "HOOKED-UP GUACAMOLE."

1 $1/2$ cups avocado
$1/3$ cup olive oil
$1/4$ cup chopped green onions
$1/2$ cup fresh cilantro, chopped
1 teaspoon minced jalapeño
1 teaspoon minced ginger
2 teaspoons minced garlic
$1/2$ cup red cherry tomatoes, diced
$1/4$ cup Nama Shoyu or 1 $1/2$ teaspoons Celtic sea salt
$1/4$ cup fresh-squeezed lime juice
1 teaspoon Juliano's Spice Chutney
$1/2$ teaspoon Mexican Spice Chutney
$1/4$ cup black sprouted rice (for recipe see page 7)
5 medium-size sunchokes, sliced into $1/4$-inch chips
2 carrots, cut into long, thin strips
1 teaspoon pomegranate seeds
a sprinkling of your favorite edible flower petals

Makes about 3 $1/2$ cups

In a bowl place avocado and olive oil and mash with a masher or wooden spoon in rapid circular strokes until fluffy. Fold in green onions, cilantro, jalapeño, ginger, garlic, tomato, Nama Shoyu or Celtic sea salt, lime juice, Juliano's Spice Chutney, and Mexican Spice Chutney. Form the guacamole into a mound in the center of a serving dish and cover it with black sprouted rice. Surround the guacamole with sunchoke chips. Place carrot strips between the chips. Sprinkle with pomegranate and flower petals. Serve.

ITALIAN GUACAMOLE

SERVE WITH RAW CHIPS, OR IN PURPLE CABBAGE OR ROMAINE LEAVES.

2 cups avocado
$1/4$ cup Nama Shoyu
1 teaspoon minced jalapeño
1 teaspoon minced ginger
1 teaspoon minced garlic
$1/2$ teaspoon Juliano's Spice Chutney
$1/4$ cup red bell pepper, diced
$1/4$ cup Marinated Portobello (for recipe see page 238)
$1/4$ cup black olives, pitted
$1/4$ cup fresh basil, chopped
2 tablespoons fresh oregano, chopped
2 tablespoons fresh rosemary, chopped
$1/2$ teaspoon fresh tarragon, chopped
$1/3$ cup marinated Sun-dried Tomatoes
   (for recipe see page 242)
$1/4$ cup Cured Eggplant (for recipe see page 237)
$1/3$ cup onions
$1/4$ cup fresh-squeezed lemon juice

Makes about 5 cups

In a bowl combine avocado, Nama Shoyu, jalapeño, ginger, garlic, and Juliano's Spice Chutney and mash until fluffy. Add red bell pepper, Marinated Portobello, black olives, basil, oregano, rosemary, tarragon, Sun-dried Tomatoes, Cured Eggplant, onions, and lemon juice.

RAW SPROUTED HUMMUS

2 cups sprouted chickpeas (a.k.a. garbanzo beans;
  for recipe see page 7)
$1/2$ cup fresh parsley, chopped
$1/4$ cup pitted black olives
$1/4$ cup fresh-squeezed lemon juice
$1/2$ teaspoon minced jalapeño
1 tablespoon minced garlic
$1/4$ cup tahini
$1/4$ to $1/2$ cup olive oil (You can never have too much!)
1 teaspoon Mexican Spice Chutney (for recipe see page 227)
$1/4$ cup Nama Shoyu or 1 $1/2$ teaspoons Celtic sea salt

Place all the above ingredients in a blender and blend until creamy,
using rubber scraper to help the hummus turn over.

SPROUTED BARLEY BABE

THINK ENERGY-CHARGED MUSHROOM AND BARLEY PILAF.

Serves 4

1 cup fresh mushrooms, diced
3 cups of any vegetables or savory fruits
  (grated zucchini or squash, diced eggplant, and/or corn kernels)
1 cup sprouted barley (for recipe see page 7)
$^1/_4$ cup minced green onions
1 $^1/_2$ teaspoons minced garlic
$^1/_2$ cup fresh-squeezed lemon juice
$^2/_3$ cup diced tomatoes
$^2/_3$ cup olive oil
1 teaspoon miso
1 teaspoon cashew butter
2 teaspoons Celtic sea salt
1 teaspoon minced jalapeño
ground black pepper to taste

Combine all the ingredients in a serving bowl.
Mix and serve.

CURRIED PÂTÉ

SERVE WITH CASHEW FLOWER CINNAMON YOGURT.

Soak the pumpkin and sunflower seeds with enough water to cover for 10 minutes. Drain and place in a serving bowl with Curry Chutney, Celtic sea salt, orange juice, avocado, onion, garlic, ginger, jalapeño, parsley, and tomato. Mix & munch.

1 cup pumpkin seeds
1 cup sunflower seeds
water for soaking seeds
1 tablespoon Curry Chutney (for recipe see page 228)
1 teaspoon Celtic sea salt
$1/2$ cup fresh-squeezed orange juice
1 avocado, cubed
$1/3$ cup chopped onion
$1/2$ tablespoon minced garlic
1 teaspoon minced ginger
1 teaspoon minced jalapeño
$1/3$ cup fresh parsley, chopped
1 cup diced tomato

Serves 4 as an appetizer

Hummus à l'Ôrange

Makes about 5 cups

BEST WHEN SERVED WITH RAW CHIPS OR FLAX SEED CRACKERS.

2 cups sprouted chickpeas
  (garbanzos, for recipe see page 7)
1 1/2 teaspoons Celtic sea salt
1/4 cup golden miso
1 cup fresh-squeezed orange juice
1/3 cup tahini
1/3 cup hemp oil (or olive oil)
1 teaspoon Mexican Spice Chutney (for recipe see page 227)
1 teaspoon minced jalapeño
1 teaspoon minced garlic
1 teaspoon minced ginger
1/3 cup fresh-squeezed lemon juice
1/2 cup honey, maple syrup, or dates
1 cup pistachios

In a blender blend the above ingredients using rubber scraper to help turn over. Serve.

HUMMUS À L'

QUINOA IS A FUSSY LITTLE GRAIN, SO TO SPROUT IT USE ONLY ENOUGH
WATER TO COVER; IT DOESN'T NEED TO SOAK, JUST TO ABSORB
ENOUGH WATER TO HELP IT GROW. IF THE QUINOA FEELS A BIT DRY
AFTER IT'S ABSORBED THE WATER ADD A LITTLE MORE. RINSE THE
GRAINS THREE TIMES THE DAY YOU INTRODUCE THEM TO WATER AND
WITHIN ONE DAY, THEY'LL SPROUT.

QUINOA TABOULEH

[KEN-wah or KEEN-wah]

This cool grain is rich in protein, potassium and phosphorus.

Serves 4

as an appetizer

$1/4$ cup sprouted quinoa
  (for recipe see page 7)
$1/2$ cup cherry tomatoes, halved
2 tablespoons Nama Shoyu or 1 $1/2$ teaspoons Celtic sea salt
$1/4$ cup fresh-squeezed lemon juice
$1/2$ cup fresh mint, chopped
$1/4$ cup diced burdock
$1/4$ cup diced cucumber
1 cup fresh parsley (including stems), chopped
1 tablespoon minced garlic
1 teaspoon minced jalapeño
1 teaspoon minced ginger
$1/2$ cup olive oil

Combine the above ingredients in a mixing bowl.
Mix and serve.

2 cups sprouted chickpeas
 (for recipe see page 7)
2 $\frac{1}{2}$ cups filtered water
$\frac{1}{4}$ cup tahini
$\frac{1}{4}$ cup sliced burdock
$\frac{1}{4}$ cup lemon juice
2 teaspoons Celtic sea salt
1 cup cherry tomatoes, halved
1 tablespoon Nama Shoyu
$\frac{2}{3}$ cup mint, chopped
$\frac{1}{3}$ cup diced cucumber
$\frac{1}{3}$ cup chopped parsley
1 tablespoon garlic
1 teaspoon minced jalapeño
1 teaspoon minced ginger
$\frac{1}{2}$ cup olive oil
1 cup sprouted quinoa
 (for recipe see page 7)

Makes about 2 cups

CREAMY QUINOA TABOULEH

In a blender combine the sprouted chickpeas and water and blend well. Pour the chickpea mix into a fine sieve over the sink. Rinse the chickpea mix and pour it back into the blender. Add the tahini, burdock, lemon juice, and Celtic sea salt and blend until creamy. Transfer the blender contents into a serving bowl and fold in the cherry tomatoes, 1 tablespoon Nama Shoyu, mint, cucumber, parsley, garlic, jalapeño, ginger, olive oil, and sprouted quinoa. Serve.

CREAMY AND LIGHT, THIS TASTE AND
COMBINATION OF FOOD SIMPLY DIDN'T EXIST
UNTIL NOW!

Serves 4

BLACK OLIVE
& CREAM DIM SUM

2 cups avocado
$1/2$ cup black olives, pitted
1 $1/2$ teaspoons Celtic sea salt
$1/3$ cup fresh cilantro or other herb(s) chopped
$1/4$ cup fresh-squeezed lemon juice
2 teaspoons cumin
$1/2$ cup onion
2 teaspoons garlic
2 teaspoons ginger
1 $1/2$ teaspoons minced jalapeño
8 red leaf lettuce leaves

In a bowl combine the avocado, olives, Celtic sea salt, cilantro or other herb(s), lemon juice, cumin, onion, garlic, ginger, and jalapeño. Spoon the mixture evenly into lettuce leaves. Seal (by rolling the leaf around the mixture) and serve.

STUFFING

Serves 4

2 cups corn
$1/3$ cup olive oil
$1/4$ cup minced onion
$1/4$ cup minced celery
$1/4$ cup shredded carrot
$1/2$ cup lemon juice
1 teaspoon minced garlic
1 teaspoon minced jalapeño
$1/2$ cup Nama Shoyu or 1 teaspoon Celtic sea salt

Combine the above ingredients in a serving bowl. Mix and serve.

SUSHI

TO MAKE SUSHI, you need to lay nori sheets with the shorter side directly in front of you on a dry, non-slippery surface such as a cutting board. Be sure to keep the nori dry!

Whichever recipe you follow, you'll have to arrange the fillings along the end closest to you, making sure to spread your filling all the way from end to end to ensure an evenly stuffed roll.

I always arrange chives, carrot sticks, green leaves, fresh horseradish, etc. so they're sticking out each end of the roll; it makes for a dramatic presentation on a sushi platter.

When the filling is in place, roll the sushi using gentle pressure, while being careful to roll the end closest to you over the filling into a snugly wrapped, firm roll. Then dip your finger tip in water and moisten the end edge of roll. (Dry hands before touching roll again.)

When you've finish rolling the sushi leave it sitting on its moistened seam and cut into pieces using a sharp serrated knife (don't *push* the knife through the roll; slice it while gripping the roll near its base).

How To Roll Sushi

SUSHI IS GREAT ALONE, BUT ADD THE FOLLOWING EDIBLE GARNISHES AND YOU'VE GOT THE MOST BEAUTIFUL, DELICIOUS SUSHI ON EARTH!

1 TEASPOON OF YOUR FAVORITE FRUIT, DICED
FRESH MINCED HORSERADISH TO TASTE

PICKLED GINGER TO TASTE (FOR RECIPE, SEE PAGE 240)
1 TEASPOON BLACK SESAME SEEDS
1 TEASPOON FRESH DILL
1 TEASPOON DICED RED BELL PEPPER
NAMA SHOYU TO TASTE

DECORATIVELY ARRANGE THE SUSHI, FRUIT, HORSE-RADISH AND PICKLED GINGER ON A SERVING PLATE. (I USUALLY USE A WOODEN CUTTING BOARD.) SPRINKLE THE ENTIRE PLATE WITH SESAME SEEDS, DILL AND RED BELL PEPPER. PLACE NAMA SHOYU IN A SMALL DISH ON YOUR SERVING PLATE. VOILA!

½ cup RAW Ricotta Cheese (for recipe see page 255)
   or Mac Cream (for recipe see page 254)
1 ½ cups carrot pulp
   (from a juicer or you can get it at most health food stores)
2 teaspoons minced garlic
2 teaspoons minced ginger
⅓ cup dill chopped
½ cup onion minced
Carrot juice, fresh pressed (as needed)
2 sheets of nori
6 fresh horseradish sticks, sliced thin
4 cucumber sticks, sliced thin
   (leave skin on cucumber; it has great texture)
6 whole chives
¼ cup Marinated Portobello (for recipe see page 238)
1 tomato wedge, sliced into thin strips
⅛ of an avocado, sliced into thin wedges
lettuce leaves, enough to cover

IT HAS A BEAUTIFUL LIGHT ORANGE COLOR, PERFECT TEXTURE, AND TASTES LIKE THE SEA.

Makes 2 rolls

MOCK SALMON

In a mixing bowl make the Mock Salmon by combining the RAW Ricotta Cheese, carrot pulp, garlic, ginger, dill, and onion and mash well (if it's dry, add a little carrot juice). Set aside.

On a sheet of nori arrange a few horseradish and cucumber sticks and chives along the edge of the nori closest to you with the ends sticking out of each end of the roll. Gently spread half the Mock Salmon on top of the vegetable sticks, being careful not to allow the mixture to touch the nori.

Add a layer of Marinated Portobello mushrooms (squeeze excess moisture from them prior to using), tomato and avocado slices and lettuce leaves (cover any wet ingredients with leaves so the nori doesn't get wet).

Roll, slice into bite-size pieces and garnish (optional, see Sushi Garnish on page 107). Repeat the process for the second roll.

2/3 cup avocado, chopped into chunks
1/4 cup sprouted quinoa
   (for recipe see page 7)
1/3 cup diced tomato
1/3 cup fresh parsley, chopped
2 teaspoons minced garlic
2 teaspoons minced ginger
2 sheets of nori
4 fresh horseradish sticks, sliced thin
4 carrot sticks, sliced thin
4 cucumber sticks, sliced thin
   (leave skin on cucumber; it has great texture)
6 whole chives
1/4 cup Marinated Portobello
   (for recipe see page 238)
4 apple slices, sliced thin
1/4 cup Mellowkraut (for recipe see page 241)
lettuce leaves, enough to cover

AVO SUSHI

Makes 2 rolls

Mix the avocado, sprouted quinoa, tomato, parsley, garlic, and ginger in a bowl. Set aside.

On a sheet of nori arrange a few horseradish, carrot, and cucumber sticks and chives along the edge of the nori closest to you with the ends sticking out of each end of the roll. Gently spread 1/3 cup of the avocado mixture over the horseradish, carrot, cucumber, and chives, and avoid letting any of it touch the nori.

Add a layer of Marinated Portobello mushrooms (squeeze excess moisture from them prior to using), apple slices, Mellowkraut, and lettuce leaves (cover any wet ingredients with leaves so the nori doesn't get wet).

Roll, slice into bite-size pieces and garnish (optional, see Sushi Garnish on page 107). Repeat the process for the second roll.

2 sheets of nori
4 fresh horseradish sticks, sliced thin
4 carrot sticks, sliced thin
4 cucumber sticks, sliced thin
  (leave skin on cucumber; it has great texture)
6 whole chives
1 recipe of RAW Ricotta Cheese (for recipe see page 253)
  or Mac Cream (for recipe see page 252)
$1/4$ cup Marinated Portobello (for recipe see page 238)
4 apple slices, sliced thin
lettuce leaves, enough to cover

CREAM SUSHI
REAL SUSHI BARS DON'T EVEN HAVE THIS ONE.

Makes 2 rolls

On a sheet of nori arrange a few horseradish, cucumber, and carrot sticks and chives along the edge of the nori closest to you with the ends sticking out of each end of the roll. Gently spread half the cream (RAW Ricotta or Mac Cream) on top of the vegetable sticks, being careful not to allow the mixture to touch the nori.

Add a layer of Marinated Portobello mushrooms (squeeze excess moisture from them prior to using), apple slices, and lettuce leaves (cover any wet ingredients with leaves so the nori doesn't get wet).

Roll, slice into bite-size pieces and garnish (optional, see Sushi Garnish on page 107). Repeat the process for the second roll.

2 sheets of nori
4 fresh horseradish sticks, sliced thin
4 carrot sticks, sliced thin
4 cucumber sticks, sliced thin (leave skin on cucumber; it has great texture)
6 whole chives
1 recipe RAW Ricotta Cheese (for recipe see page 255)
$1/_4$ cup Marinated Portobello (for recipe see page 238)
4 apple slices, sliced into thin strips
$1/_4$ cup Mellowkraut (for recipe see page 241)
lettuce leaves, enough to cover

Makes **2** rolls

MOCK TOFU

On a sheet of nori arrange a few horseradish, cucumber and carrot sticks and chives along the edge of the nori closest to you with the ends sticking out of each end of the roll. Gently spread half of the RAW Ricotta Cheese on top of the vegetable sticks, being careful not to allow the mixture to touch the nori.

Add a layer of Marinated Portobello mushrooms (squeeze excess moisture from them prior to using), apple slices, Mellowkraut, and lettuce leaves (cover any wet ingredients with leaves so the nori doesn't get wet).

Roll, slice into bite-size pieces and garnish (optional, see Sushi Garnish on page 107). Repeat the process for the second roll.

OFU

FOR FILLING:

$2/3$ cup avocado, chopped into chunks

$1/4$ cup sprouted quinoa
  (for recipe see page 7)

$1/3$ cup diced tomato

$1/3$ cup fresh parsley, chopped

2 teaspoons minced garlic

2 teaspoons minced ginger

FOR SUSHI:

2 sheets of nori

4 fresh horseradish sticks, sliced thin

4 carrot sticks, sliced thin

4 cucumber sticks, sliced thin
  (leave skin on cucumber; it has great texture)

6 chives

$1/4$ cup Marinated Portobello (for recipe see page 238)

$1/4$ cup Cured Eggplant (for recipe see page 237)

4 apple slices, sliced thin

$1/4$ cup Mellowkraut (for recipe see page 241)

lettuce leaves, enough to cover

AVO MICRO ORGANISM

Makes 2 rolls

Mix "filling" ingredients in a bowl. Set aside. On a sheet of nori arrange a few horseradish, cucumber and carrot sticks and chives along the edge of the nori closest to you with the ends sticking out of each end of the roll. Gently spread the filling on top of the vegetable sticks, being careful not to allow the mixture to touch the nori.

Add a layer of Marinated Portobello (squeeze excess moisture from them prior to using), Cured Eggplant, apple slices, Mellowkraut, and lettuce leaves (cover any wet ingredients with leaves so the nori doesn't get wet).

Roll, slice into bite-size pieces and garnish (optional, see Sushi Garnish on page 107). Repeat the process for the second roll.

Makes **2** rolls
CAVIAR SUSHI

2 sheets of nori
4 fresh horseradish sticks, sliced thin
4 carrot sticks, sliced thin
4 cucumber sticks, sliced thin
  (leave skin on cucumber; it has great texture)
6 whole chives
$1/_4$ cup of your choice of blackberries, blueberries, raspberries, or
  pomegranate seeds or marinated papaya seeds (see Marinated
  Caviar recipe on page 83 for directions)
1 recipe Raw Ricotta Cheese (for recipe see page 255)
  or Mac Cream (for recipe see page 254)
4 apple slices, sliced thin
$1/_4$ cup Mellowkraut (for recipe see page 241)
lettuce leaves, enough to cover

On a sheet of nori arrange a few horseradish, cucumber and carrot sticks and chives along the edge of the nori closest to you with the ends sticking out of each end of the roll. Gently spread RAW Ricotta Cheese or Mac Cream and $1/_4$ cup caviar on top of the vegetable sticks, being careful not to allow the mixture to touch the nori.

Add a layer of apple slices, Mellowkraut, and lettuce leaves (cover any wet ingredients with leaves so the nori doesn't get wet).

Roll, slice into bite-size pieces and garnish (optional, see Sushi Garnish on page 107). Repeat the process for the second roll.

Makes 2 rolls

MEX SUSHI

FOR FILLING:

2/3 cup avocado, chopped into chunks
1/4 cup sprouted quinoa
    (for recipe see page 7)
1/3 cup chopped tomato
1/2 cup fresh cilantro, chopped
2 teaspoons minced garlic
2 teaspoons minced ginger
1 teaspoon minced jalapeño
1 tablespoon Mexican Spice Chutney
    (for recipe see page 227)

FOR SUSHI:

2 sheets of nori
4 fresh horseradish sticks, sliced thin
2/3 cup shredded carrot
4 carrot sticks, sliced thin
6 whole chives
lettuce leaves, enough to cover

Combine "filling" ingredients in a bowl and mix well. Set aside.

On a sheet of nori arrange some shredded carrot and a few horseradish and carrot sticks and chives along the edge of the nori closest to you with the ends sticking out of each end of the roll. Gently spread the filling on top of the vegetable sticks, being careful not to allow the mixture to touch the nori.

Add a layer of lettuce leaves (enough to cover any wet ingredients with leaves so the nori doesn't get wet).

Roll, slice into bite-size pieces and garnish (optional, see Sushi Garnish on page 107). Repeat the process for the second roll.

Makes **2** rolls

MUSHROOM CREAM SUSHI

FOR FILLING:
1 recipe RAW Ricotta Cheese (for recipe see page 255)
  or Mac Cream (for recipe see page 254)

FOR SUSHI:
2 sheets of nori
4 fresh horseradish sticks, sliced thin
4 carrot sticks
4 cucumber sticks, sliced thin
  (leave skin on cucumber; it has great texture)
1 cup sliced mushrooms
6 chives
4 apple slices, sliced thin
lettuce leaves, enough to cover

On a sheet of nori arrange a few horseradish, cucumber and carrot sticks, mushrooms and chives along the edge of the nori closest to you with the ends sticking out of each end of the roll. Gently spread selected filling on top of the vegetable sticks, being careful not to allow the mixture to touch the nori.

Add a layer of apple slices, and lettuce leaves (cover any wet ingredients with leaves so the nori doesn't get wet).

Roll, slice into bite-size pieces and garnish (optional, see Sushi Garnish on page 107). Repeat the process for the second roll.

Makes **2** pieces
PORTOBELLO, MANGO, OR PAPAYA NIGIRI

1 sheet of nori, cut lengthwise into long 1-inch-wide strips
2 wedges avocado, about $1/_2$-inch thick
2 wedge-shaped slices of portobello mushroom,
   mango, or papaya, about $1/_2$-inch thick
4 fresh horseradish sticks, sliced thin
2 apple slices
4 cucumber sticks, sliced thin
4 carrot sticks, sliced thin
4 whole chives

Lay a long nori strip onto a clean surface. Place an avocado wedge on the nori. (The strip should be perpendicular to the avocado, making a "+".) Add a slice of mushroom, mango, or papaya, and horseradish, apple, carrot, and cucumber sticks, and chives. Wrap the nori tightly around the stacked ingredients and seal the two ends together with a little water. Serve the nigiri on a wooden board or a plate. Garnish is optional, see Sushi Garnish on page 107.

FOR COLORING (OPTIONAL):
3 medium beets (for $1/2$ cup fresh beet juice),
   1 pound carrots (for 1 cup fresh carrot juice),
   or 4 shots wheatgrass juice

FOR SUSHI:
2 aloe slices, cut into a $1/2$-inch wedge
1 sheet of nori, cut lengthwise into long 1-inch-wide strips
2 wedges avocado, about $1/2$-inch thick
2 apple slices, cut into thin strips
4 fresh horseradish sticks, sliced thin
6 cucumber sticks, sliced thin
6 carrot sticks, sliced thin
6 whole chives

ALOE NIGIRI

I make a variety of colorful nigiri by taking pieces of aloe and dyeing them with natural juices. It's not necessary to dye the aloe to enjoy the dish, but should you choose to go for it, you have three selections: beet juice for Mock Tuna, carrot juice for Mock Salmon, and wheatgrass juice for Alien Sushi.

If you plan to dye the aloe, begin this recipe by juicing your selected dyes in a juicer. You can also buy them at a health food store. Then soak the aloe in the juice for 5 or 10 minutes. Set aside.

Lay a long strip of nori on a clean surface. Place an avocado wedge on the nori. (The strip should be perpendicular to the avocado, making a "+".) Add a slice of horseradish, apple, carrot and cucumber sticks, and chives. Top with aloe slices. Wrap the nori tightly around the stacked ingredients and seal the two ends together with a little water.

Serve the nigiri on a plate. Garnish is optional, see Sushi Garnish on page 107.

Makes 2 pieces

IGIRI

Use large aloe leaves for this recipe. Small aloe leaves tend to be bitter; big leaves are more tasteless, which in this case is ideal.

7

PIZZA

SICILIAN

SICILIAN PIZZA

For an instant feast, use romaine lettuce leaves as the base for any of the pizzas if you're out of Living Buckwheat Crust. Wrap pizza ingredients in lettuce leaves and crunch and munch.

1 10-inch Living Buckwheat Pizza Crust (for recipe see page 52)
2 cups Avo Chutney (for recipe see page 230)
$1/_4$ cup cherry tomatoes, halved
$1/_4$ cup Cured Eggplant, chopped (for recipe see page 237)
$1/_4$ cup fresh basil, chopped
2 teaspoons fresh rosemary
$1/_2$ cup sun-dried tomatoes, chopped
1 teaspoon fresh oregano, chopped
1 cup Marinated Portobello, chopped (for recipe see page 238)
$1/_2$ cup scallions, chopped
$1/_3$ cup red bell pepper, chopped
$1/_3$ cup black olives, pitted and chopped
1 teaspoon edible flower petals (optional)
$1/_2$ lemon

On a Living Buckwheat Crust spread Avo Chutney almost double the thickness of the crust and layer with the remaining ingredients in the following order (for dramatic color and presentation): cherry tomatoes, Cured Eggplant, basil, rosemary, and sun-dried tomatoes. Serve on a small cutting board or decorative plate and garnish with oregano, Marinated Portobello, scallions, red bell pepper, olives, and flower petals. Finish it off with a good sprinkling of fresh-squeezed lemon!

SAMURAI PIZZA

AS ONE WISE FRIEND SAID TO ME OVER A SAMURAI PIZZA LUNCH, "IT'S SO GOOD I DON'T WANT TO RUIN IT BY CALLING IT PIZZA."

1 10-inch Living Buckwheat Pizza Crust
   (for recipe see page 52)
2 cups Avo Chutney (for recipe see page 230)
$1/2$ cup salad mix, chopped
1 tablespoon organic raisins
$1/4$ cup diced cucumbers
$1/2$ cup Mellowkraut (for recipe see page 241)
$1/2$ tablespoon minced dill
1 tablespoon pine nuts
1 tablespoon chopped scallions
1 teaspoon edible flowers (optional)
$1/4$ cup red bell pepper, finely chopped
2 tablespoons pickled ginger
$1/2$ lemon

Serves 2

On a Living Buckwheat Crust spread Avo Chutney almost double the thickness of the crust and layer with the remaining ingredients in the following order (for dramatic color and presentation): salad mix, raisins, cucumbers, Mellowkraut, dill, pine nuts, and scallions. Serve on a small cutting board or decorative plate and sprinkle with edible flower petals and red bell pepper. Garnish with pickled ginger and finish off with a generous sprinkling of fresh-squeezed lemon.

Serves 2

1 10-inch Living Buckwheat Crust (for recipe see page 52)
1 recipe Mac Cream (for recipe see page 254)
 or RAW Ricotta Cheese (for recipe see page 255)
2 cups Exquisite RAW Marinara (for recipe see page 219)
$1/2$ cup chopped tomatoes
$1/2$ cup fresh basil, chopped
2 teaspoons fresh oregano, chopped
2 teaspoons fresh tarragon, chopped
2 teaspoons fresh rosemary, de-stemmed and chopped
$1/2$ cup Cured Eggplant (for recipe see page 237)
$1/3$ cup Sun-dried Tomato (for recipe see page 242)
1 tablespoon minced jalapeño
4 tablespoons Marinated Portobello (for recipe see page 238)
1 tablespoon chopped scallions
1 tablespoon red bell pepper, chopped
1 tablespoon chopped black olives
1 tablespoon of your favorite edible flowers
$1/2$ lemon

ITALIAN PIZZA

On a Living Buckwheat Crust spread Mac Cream or Raw Ricotta and top with the following ingredients in the order listed (for dramatic color): RAW Marinara, tomatoes, basil, oregano, tarragon, rosemary, Cured Eggplant (arranged the way you like it), and Sun-dried Tomato. Garnish with jalapeño, Marinated Portabello, scallions, bell pepper, olives, and flowers. Finish it off with a good sprinkling of fresh-squeezed lemon!

Serves 2
LEBANESE PIZZA

1 10-inch Living Buckwheat Pizza Crust
  (for recipe see page 52)
1 recipe of RAW Sprouted Hummus
  (for recipe see page 94)
2 recipes of Creamy Quinoa Tabouleh
  (for recipe see page 100)
$1/4$ cup black olives, pitted and chopped
$1/2$ cup red bell pepper, diced

On a Living Buckwheat Crust spread RAW
Sprouted Hummus, about double the thickness
of the crust. Add a layer about half as thick as
the Hummus of Creamy Quinoa Tabouleh.
Serve on a small cutting board and garnish with
black olives and red bell pepper.

PIZZA

1 10-inch Living Buckwheat Pizza Crust
  (for recipe see page 52)
1 cup RAW Pesto Sauce (for recipe see page 220)
1 1/2 cup Exquisite RAW Marinara Sauce
  (optional; for recipe see page 219)
1 cup salad mix (your favorite lettuces)
1/2 cup Cured Eggplant, chopped (for recipe see page 237)
2/3 cup sun-dried tomatoes, chopped
1 1/2 teaspoons fresh oregano, chopped
1 teaspoon fresh tarragon, chopped
1 1/2 teaspoons fresh rosemary, chopped
1/4 cup chopped tomatoes
1 teaspoon minced jalapeño
1 cup Marinated Portobello (for recipe see page 238)
1/2 cup scallions, chopped
1/3 cup red bell pepper, chopped
1/3 cup green olives, pitted and chopped
1 teaspoon edible flower petals (optional)
1/2 lemon

Place Living Buckwheat Crust on a small cutting board or decorative plate and spread with RAW Pesto Sauce about double the thickness of the crust. Top with the remaining ingredients in the following order (for dramatic color and presentation): Exquisite RAW Marinara, salad mix, Cured Eggplant, and sun-dried tomatoes. Sprinkle the pizza with oregano, tarragon, rosemary, tomatoes, jalapeño, Marinated Portobello, scallions, red bell pepper, green olives, and flower petals (optional). Finish it off with a good sprinkling of fresh-squeezed lemon.

PESTO PIZZA

Serves 2

I HAVE A FRIEND WHOSE KIDS LOVE PIZZA FOR BREAKFAST.
SHE GUILTLESSLY SERVES THEM THIS ONE, WHICH IS MY VERSION OF FRUIT AND
WHIPPED CREAM ON CRISPY PIE CRUST.

3 tablespoons olive oil
2 cups avocado
$1/2$ cup maple syrup
$1/2$ teaspoon Juliano's Spice Chutney (for recipe see page 227)
1 $1/2$ teaspoons Celtic sea salt or 1 tablespoon Nama Shoyu
$1/2$ teaspoon minced jalapeño
1 teaspoon minced ginger
$1/2$ teaspoon minced garlic
$1/3$ cup raw almond butter
1 10-inch Living Buckwheat Crust (for recipe see page 52)
$1/2$ cup dates, pitted and chopped
$1/2$ cup banana, sliced
$1/2$ cup strawberries, sliced
$1/2$ cup kiwi, peeled and sliced
$1/4$ cup fresh minced coconut
$1/4$ cup of your favorite berries
$1/4$ cup chopped mint leaves
1 teaspoon of your favorite edible flower petals (optional)
$1/2$ lemon

TROPICAL PIZZA Serves 2
(A.K.A. KIDS' PIZZA

In a mixing bowl whip olive oil and avocado for about one minute with a large fork, until it resembles a fluffy cream. Add the maple syrup, Juliano's Spice Chutney, Celtic sea salt or Nama Shoyu, jalapeño, ginger, garlic, and almond butter. Spread the mixture on a Living Buckwheat Crust and top with the following ingredients in the following order for dramatic color: a layer of dates, banana, strawberries and kiwi. You can substitute any of your favorite fruits. Sprinkle the pizza with fresh minced coconut, berries, chopped mint leaves and flower petals, and lemon juice, and serve on a small cutting board or decorative plate.

3 tablespoons olive oil

2 cups avocado

1 teaspoon Mexican Spice Chutney
 (for recipe see page 227)

1 teaspoon Juliano's Spice Chutney
 (for recipe see page 227)

3 tablespoons Nama Shoyu or 1 $\frac{1}{2}$ teaspoons Celtic sea salt

1 teaspoon minced jalapeño

2 teaspoons minced garlic

1 teaspoon minced ginger

1 10-inch Living Buckwheat Crust
 (for recipe see page 52)

$\frac{1}{2}$ cup fresh cilantro, chopped

$\frac{1}{2}$ cup diced tomato

$\frac{1}{4}$ cup mango, julienne (mango can be substituted with
 pineapple, strawberries or kiwi and/or any other fruit)

$\frac{1}{4}$ cup minced coconut

$\frac{1}{4}$ cup red bell pepper, diced

$\frac{1}{4}$ cup scallions

$\frac{1}{4}$ cup green olives, pitted and chopped

1 teaspoon of your favorite edible flower petals

1 lime

Serves 2

AVO MANGO PIZZA
MEXICAN BLISS!

In a mixing bowl whip olive oil and avocado for about one minute with a large fork, until it resembles a fluffy cream. Add the Mexican Spice Chutney, Juliano's Spice Chutney, Nama Shoyu or Celtic sea salt, jalapeño, garlic, and ginger. The mixture should be a little too salty and spicy because many mild ingredients will go on top of this pizza. Spread mixture on the Living Buckwheat Crust and top with the following ingredients in the order listed for the best presentation: cilantro, tomato, and mango or other selected fruit. Serve on a small cutting board and sprinkle with freshly minced coconut, red bell pepper, scallions, green olives and flower petals. Drizzle fresh-squeezed lime over the pizza and serve.

3 tablespoons olive oil

2 cups avocado

1 teaspoon Mexican Spice Chutney (for recipe see page 227)

1 teaspoon Juliano's Spice Chutney (for recipe see page 227)

$1/4$ cup Nama Shoyu or 1 $1/2$ teaspoons Celtic sea salt

1 $1/2$ teaspoons minced jalapeño

1 tablespoon minced garlic

1 tablespoon minced ginger

1 10-inch Living Buckwheat Crust

$1/2$ cup fresh cilantro, chopped

$1/2$ cup diced tomatoes

$1/2$ cup corn, cut from the cob

$1/2$ cup carrots, diced

$1/2$ cup peas

$1/4$ cup freshly minced coconut

$1/4$ cup red bell pepper, diced

$1/4$ cup chopped scallions

1 tablespoon of your favorite edible flower petals (optional)

1 lime

Serves 2

AMERICAN PIZZA

In a mixing bowl whip olive oil and avocado for about one minute with a large fork, until it resembles a fluffy cream. Add the Mexican Spice Chutney, Juliano's Spice Chutney, Nama Shoyu or Celtic sea salt, jalapeño, garlic, and ginger. The mixture should be just a little too salty and spicy because many mild ingredients will go on top of this pizza. Spread the mixture on a Living Buckwheat Crust about double the thickness of the crust. Top the pizza with cilantro and tomatoes and sprinkle with corn, carrots, peas, freshly minced coconut, red bell pepper, scallions and flower petals. Finish the pizza with a fresh squeeze of lime.

P

1 cup banana, sliced
1 cup avocado
1 $1/3$ cups raw almond butter
1 $1/2$ teaspoons Celtic sea salt
1 $1/2$ teaspoons minced jalapeño
1 teaspoon minced ginger
$1/2$ teaspoon minced garlic, optional
1 teaspoon Juliano's Spice Chutney
  (for recipe see page 227)
1 10-inch Living Buckwheat Crust
  (for recipe see page 52)
$1/2$ cup soft dates, chopped
$1/2$ cup strawberries, sliced
$1/2$ cup kiwi, sliced
$1/4$ cup fresh minced coconut
$1/4$ cup of your favorite berries
$1/4$ cup mint leaves, chopped
1 teaspoon of your favorite edible flower petals (optional)
$1/2$ lemon

ANOTHER GREAT ONE FOR YOUNG KIDS. Serves 2

BANANA PIZZA

In a mixing bowl mash together the banana, avocado, almond butter, Nama Shoyu or Celtic sea salt, jalapeño, ginger, garlic (optional), and Juliano's Spice Chutney. Spread the banana mixture on a Living Buckwheat Crust and layer with the following ingredients in the order listed for the most dramatic presentation: dates, strawberries, and kiwi. Serve on a small cutting board and sprinkle the pizza with fresh minced coconut, berries, chopped mint leaves, and flower petals and finish it off with a drizzle of fresh-squeezed lemon.

ZZA

MAIN COURSES

8

FOR CHEESE BURGER:
1 cup walnuts, soaked
1 cup almonds, soaked
1 cup portobello mushrooms, chopped
$1/2$ cup grated carrot
1 tablespoon white miso
$1/4$ cup minced onion
2 tablespoons Nama Shoyu or 2 teaspoons Celtic sea salt
1 teaspoon coriander, ground
1 teaspoon Mexican Spice Chutney (for recipe see page 227)
$2/3$ cup seaweed water, or vegetable juice

ANCILLARY GOODIES:
2 slices Nacho Cheese (for recipe see page 259)
4 slices Real Toast (for recipe see page 61)
Ketchup (for recipe see page 243)
Mayo #1 or #2 (for recipes see page 245)
mustard, to taste
pickles, to taste
onions, to taste
romaine leaves or sprouts, to taste
tomato slices, to taste
avocado, sliced

Serves 2

CHEESE BURGER #1

In a food processor, puree nuts, mushrooms, and carrots. Add the remaining ingredients and puree. Form the mixture into 2 4-inch patties on a mesh dehydrator sheet. Dehydrate the patties for 8 hours at 90°F. Remove the patties from the dehydrator, top them with Nacho Cheese slices, and dehydrate for 2 more hours. Place each patty between two pieces of Real Toast and add your favorite combination of Ketchup, Mayo #1 or #2, mustard, pickles, onions, romaine leaves or sprouts, tomato, and avocado.

Serves 6
GORDON'S FISH PATTIES

3 medium rutabagas
3 cloves garlic, minced
$^{1}/_{2}$ tablespoon Celtic sea salt
$^{1}/_{4}$ cup olive oil
1 tablespoon scallions or grated onion

In a food processor, puree the rutabagas, garlic, salt, and olive oil (it should have a granular consistency). Form the potato mixture into 4-inch patties on mesh dehydrator sheet. Sprinkle with scallions or grated onion. Dehydrate for 10 hours at 90°F.

TTIES

1 medium beet (for $^1/_2$ cup beet pulp)
$^1/_4$ pound carrots (for $^1/_2$ cup carrot pulp)
1 tablespoon black miso
$^1/_2$ cup portobello mushrooms, chopped
1 $^1/_2$ teaspoons minced garlic
1 tablespoon olive oil
4 $^1/_2$ teaspoons Nama Shoyu or 1 $^1/_2$ teaspoons Celtic sea salt
$^1/_4$ cup fresh-squeezed orange juice
2 slices Nacho Cheese (for recipes see page 259)
4 slices Real Toast (for recipe see page 61)
Ketchup (for recipe see page 243)
Mayo #1 or #2 (for recipes see page 245)
mustard, to taste
pickles, to taste
onions, to taste
romaine leaves or sprouts, to taste
avocado, sliced
tomato slices, to taste

WITH FRENCH FRIES, CREAMY COLE SLAW, AND A MILK SHAKE, IT CAN'T BE BEAT. Serves 2

CHEESE BURGER #2

With a juicer, juice the beet and carrots until you have $^1/_2$ cup of beet pulp and $^1/_2$ cup of carrot pulp. Drink the juice! If you don't have a juicer, buy the pulp at a health food store. In a mixing bowl combine the beet pulp, carrot pulp, and black miso. Set aside.

In a blender or blender jar combine portobello mushrooms, garlic, olive oil, and Nama Shoyu or Celtic sea salt and blend into a cream; add orange juice sparingly if mixture is too thick to blend. Add the blender contents to the pulp mixture and mash the ingredients together.

Form the mash into 2 4-inch patties and dehydrate them at 90°F for 2 hours. Remove the patties from the dehydrator, top them with Nacho Cheese slices, and continue dehydrating for 1 or 2 hours.

Place each patty between two pieces of Real Toast and add your favorite combination of Ketchup, Mayo #1 or #2, mustard, pickles, onions, romaine leaves or sprouts, avocado, and tomato.

1 $1/3$ cups walnuts

1 $1/3$ cups sunflower seeds

1 $1/3$ cups almonds

filtered water for soaking sunflower seeds and almonds

1 tablespoon minced garlic

$1/2$ tablespoon Celtic sea salt

$1/2$ cup fresh parsley, chopped

$1/2$ cup chopped celery

2 cups Marinated Portobello, chopped
(for recipe see page 238)

1 tablespoon chopped onion

$1/2$ tablespoon minced ginger

2 tablespoons fresh rosemary, de-stemmed and minced

1 tablespoon fresh tarragon, minced

1 cup red bell pepper, chopped

1 tablespoon minced jalapeño

1 $1/2$ teaspoons cumin seeds (not powder)

$1/2$ cup olive oil

1 recipe Barbecue Sauce
(for recipe see page 216)

Soak sunflower seeds and almonds in enough water to cover for 2 to 6 hours. Soak walnuts for $1/2$ hour. Drain and throw the nuts and seeds into a food processor with the minced garlic. If you have a Green Power, push them through—they're best when homogenized. Process until the contents develop a dough-like consistency. Add a dash of olive oil if the dough is too thick. Stir in the Celtic sea salt, parsley, celery, Marinated Portobello, onion, ginger, rosemary, tarragon, red bell pepper, jalapeño, cumin seeds, and olive oil. Mix well. On a solid dehydrating sheet shape the mixture into a loaf about $1 1/2$ inches high. Dehydrate for 1 hour at 90°F. Remove the loaf from the dehydrator and baste it with Barbecue Sauce. Dehydrate for 2 to 3 more hours at 90°F. Serve immediately.

FOR CRUST:

2 cups ground walnuts or almonds

2 tablespoons seaweed water or filtered water

FOR FILLING:

1 cup vegetable pulp
  (from a 2 pound combo of carrot, broccoli,
  cauliflower, red bell pepper, yam, or celery)

1 cup cashews

water for soaking cashews

1 $1/2$ cups sprouted sunflower seeds
  (for recipe see page 7)

$1/2$ cup vegetable juice

$1/4$ cup Nama Shoyu or 1 teaspoon Celtic sea salt

2 tablespoons fresh-squeezed lemon juice

1 cup chopped broccoli

$1/2$ cup chopped onion

Serves 2

RAW POT PIE

Soak cashews in water for at least 1 hour. Drain and set aside. In a juicer, juice the vegetable combo until you have 1 cup of vegetable pulp and $1/2$ cup vegetable juice. If you don't have a juicer you can purchase the juice and pulp at a health food store.

Make the crust: in a bowl mix 1 cup of the nuts and water together. Kneed the mixture into dough and divide the dough into quarters. Press one quarter of the dough into a small 6-inch soup bowl; repeat the procedure with a second soup bowl. Shape the remaining two quarters into two circles the same diameter of the soup bowl and place them on a solid dehydrator sheet. Place the bowls and the dehydrator sheet in a dehydrator and dehydrate at 90°F for 8 hours.

In a food processor combine the vegetable pulp, soaked cashews, 1 cup sunflower seeds, vegetable juice, Nama Shoyu or Celtic sea salt, and lemon juice. Blend until smooth. Pour the mixture into a mixing bowl and fold in the broccoli, onion, and the remaining $1/2$ cup of sunflower seeds. Spoon the pot pie filling into crust-filled soup bowl and top it with small circle crust.

2 cups sprouted black beans
  (for recipe see page 7) or Raw Hummus (for recipe see page 94)
$^1/_4$ cup olive oil
$^1/_4$ cup diced tomato
$^1/_2$ medium red bell pepper
$^1/_4$ cup Nama Shoyu or 1 $^1/_2$ teaspoons Celtic sea salt
2 whole green or purple cabbage leaves, without tears
$^2/_3$ cup fresh cilantro, chopped
2 tablespoons RAW Salsa (for recipe see page 232) or Cilantro
  Salsa (for recipe see page 233)
2 tablespoons Guacamole (for recipe see page 88)
$^1/_2$ cup cherry tomatoes, halved

Serves 2

RAW REFRIED BEANS
AND RICE BURRITOS

In a food processor combine the black
beans, olive oil, tomato, red bell pepper,
and Nama Shoyu or Celtic sea salt and
blend until mixed, but coarse. Spread the
beans evenly into each of the cabbage
leaves (use a limp one if you prefer a soft
tortilla to a crunchy one) and add
cilantro, RAW Salsa or Cilantro Salsa,
Guacamole, and cherry tomatoes. Wrap
the sides of each cabbage leaf around its
contents and eat.

LAST MINUTE BURRITOS

1/4 cup fresh mint, chopped

2 cups avocado, diced

1/4 cup Nama Shoyu or 1 1/2 teaspoons Celtic sea salt

1/4 cup chopped onion

1 tablespoon fresh rosemary, chopped

1 1/2 teaspoons Curry Chutney (for recipe see page 228)

1 teaspoon cumin

2 teaspoons powdered or 1/4 cup fresh kelp

2 teaspoons powdered or 1/4 cup fresh dulce

1/4 cup lime juice

1 teaspoon minced jalapeño

4 large romaine lettuce leaves

Mix all but the romaine in a bowl. Spoon equal portions of the avocado mixture into the lettuce leaves. Wrap the leaves around the mixture and eat.

4 whole purple cabbage leaves, without tears
1 cup RAW Sprouted Hummus (for recipe see page 94)
1 $\frac{1}{2}$ cups fresh mint, chopped
$\frac{1}{2}$ medium avocado, cut into 4 slices
1 tablespoon fresh parsley, chopped
$\frac{1}{4}$ cup cherry tomatoes, halved
2 tablespoons diced cucumber
$\frac{1}{4}$ cup Marinated Onion Ringlets (for recipe see page 238)
10 black dried olives (the wrinkly ones), pitted and halved
1 tablespoon Buckwheaties (optional; for recipe see page 231)
$\frac{1}{4}$ cup RAW House Dressing (for recipe see page 212)
2 teaspoons minced Jalapeño
4 teaspoons Nama Shoyu or 1 teaspoon Celtic sea salt
1 recipe Falafel Patties (for recipe see page 65)

Serves 4

PHENOMENAL
FALAFEL BURRITOS

Assemble your falafel burrito by peeling a purple cabbage leaf from the bottom, taking care to not tear the leaf, and spreading $\frac{1}{4}$ cup RAW Sprouted Hummus across each leaf. To each leaf add equal portions of avocado, mint, parsley, cherry tomatoes, cucumber, Marinated Onions, dried olives, Buckwheaties, RAW House Dressing, jalapeño, Nama Shoyu or Celtic sea salt, and 1 Falafel Patty. Wrap the sides of each cabbage leaf around its contents and eat.

PURPLE BLUEBERRY AND RASPBERRY BURRITOS

GUARANTEED TO CURE EVEN THE MOST SERIOUS OF MEXICAN CRAVINGS.

2 purple cabbage leaves, without tears
$1/_2$ cup RAW Ricotta Cheese
   (optional; for recipe see page 255)
$1/_4$ cup Marinated Portobello
   (for recipe see page 238)
$1/_4$ cup RAW Salsa (for recipe see page 232)
$1/_4$ cup Curried Guacamole (for recipe see page 88)
$1/_4$ cup sprouted rice (optional; for recipe see page 7)
6 blueberries
6 raspberries
2 tablespoons of your choice of chopped mango,
   kiwi, or strawberry (optional)
2 teaspoons Nama Shoyu or 1 teaspoon Celtic sea salt

Peel a purple cabbage leaf from the bottom, taking care to not tear leaf. Spread RAW Ricotta Cheese inside the leaf and add Marinated Portobello, RAW Salsa, and Curried Guacamole. Top with a sprinkle of sprouted rice (optional), blueberries, raspberries, selected fruits, and Nama Shoyu or Celtic sea salt. Wrap the sides of each leaf around its contents and eat.

Neptune Burritos

FOR THE FOOD PROCESSOR:

$1/3$ cup walnuts

water for soaking walnuts

4 ounces sea palm fronds

4 ounces wakame seaweed

water for soaking palm fronds and wakame

2 celery stalks, chopped

1 cup chopped carrot

1 tablespoon scallions, chopped

1 tablespoon fresh cilantro, chopped

$1/4$ cup chopped red bell pepper

1 teaspoon Thai chili or jalapeño, minced

2 teaspoons minced garlic

2 teaspoons minced ginger

2 tablespoons shallots

$1/4$ cup Nama Shoyu

$1/4$ cup fresh-squeezed lemon juice

$1/2$ cup olive oil

2 teaspoons Umeboshi paste

FOR THE FINAL TOUCHES:

6 large romaine lettuce leaves

2 cups fresh mint leaves

$1/4$ cup shredded or chopped burdock

2 cups wakame seaweed

$1/2$ cup grated carrot

2 tablespoons scallions diced

$1/4$ bell pepper, diced small

2 tablespoons fresh cilantro, chopped fine

1 recipe of Sweet & Sour Sauce
  (for recipe see page 218)
  or Peanut Sauce (for recipe see page 217)

Serves 2

Soak the walnuts in enough water to cover for at least 2 hours and drain. Soak the palm fronds and wakame seaweed for 15 minutes and drain. Keep the seaweed water; it's a great broth and recommended in many other recipes. Place all ingredients listed in for the food processor in a food processor and puree. Spoon the blended mixture evenly into the romaine leaves (i.e., your burrito wrappers) and sprinkle even amounts of mint leaves, burdock, wakame seaweed, carrot, scallions, red bell pepper, and cilantro. Arrange decoratively on a platter and serve with either Sweet & Sour Sauce or Peanut Sauce.

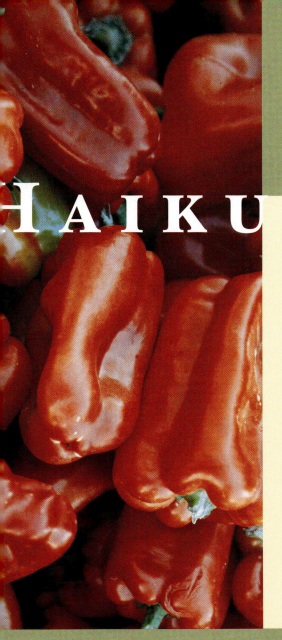

HAIKU

JAPANESE BURRITOS — RIGHT ON!

HAIKU Serves 2
BURRITOS

1 cup mashed avocado
2 teaspoons minced jalapeño
2 teaspoons minced garlic
2 teaspoons minced ginger
2 teaspoons fresh-squeezed lemon juice
2 large romaine lettuce leaves
2 teaspoons organic stone-ground mustard
1 pickle, sliced lengthwise into strips
  or $1/4$ cup Mellowkraut
  (for recipe see page 241)
$1/3$ cup wakame seaweed, thinly sliced
$1/2$ cup burdock, grated
$1/3$ cup chopped onion
$1/3$ cup red bell pepper, chopped
$1/4$ cup corn kernels, cut from the cob
2 tablespoons Nama Shoyu

In a mixing bowl, stir together the avocado, jalapeño, garlic, ginger and lemon juice. On each lettuce leaf smear half the avocado mixture, mustard, pickle or Mellowkraut, seaweed, burdock, onion, red bell pepper, corn and Nama Shoyu. Wrap like a burrito, hold like a taco, and devour.

BELLA BURRITOS

FOR VEGGIE MARINADE:
1 cup chopped mushrooms
$2/3$ cup Nama Shoyu
1 cup diced red bell pepper
$2/3$ cup diced tomato
1 $1/2$ tablespoons minced garlic
1 teaspoon minced ginger
1 tablespoon minced jalapeño
$1/2$ cup olive oil
$2/3$ cup chopped onion
$1/4$ cup fresh-squeezed lemon juice
$1/4$ cup fresh basil, chopped
1 tablespoon fresh rosemary, chopped
1 teaspoon fresh oregano, chopped
1 teaspoon fresh tarragon, chopped
1 $1/2$ tablespoons black olives,
   pitted and chopped
$1/4$ cup sun-dried tomato, chopped

Serves 4

FOR THE TABLE:
12 large romaine lettuce leaves
1 recipe Cilantro Pesto (for recipe see page 221)
2 cups shaved (with vegetable peeler) zucchini
$1/4$ cup Cured Eggplant, chopped
   (optional; for recipe see page 231)

In a serving bowl combine Veggie Marinade ingredients and mix well. Set aside for at least 10 minutes. On a serving plate arrange whole romaine leaves in a decorative fashion. Put Cilantro Pesto, shaved zucchini, and Cured Eggplant (optional) in separate serving bowls. Place the lettuce plate, Veggie Marinade, Cilantro Pesto, and shaved zucchini at the table and allow your guests to build their own Bella Burritos.

RAW SPRING ROLLS

Serves 3

1 ½ cups coconut water, seaweed water,
  or filtered water
1 tablespoon fresh-squeezed lemon juice
1 teaspoon Umeboshi paste (optional)
1 tablespoon cashew butter
1 cup walnuts
1 tablespoon golden miso
  (the color is secondary to the miso being raw)
½ tablespoon Curry Chutney (for recipe see page 228)
¼ cup chopped onion
1 medium to large cauliflower, chopped
¼ cup olive oil
3 celery stalks
½ cup chopped red onion
2 teaspoons fresh dill, de-stemmed
1 tablespoon minced garlic
2 teaspoons minced ginger
1 teaspoon minced jalapeño
1 tablespoon Nama Shoyu
1 tablespoon lime zest
6 large romaine lettuce leaves
1 ½ cups fresh mint leaves, chopped
1 cup chopped burdock
1 recipe Sweet & Sour Sauce (for recipe see page 218)

In a blender combine selected water or juice, lemon juice, Umeboshi paste (optional), cashew butter, walnuts, golden miso, Curry Chutney, and ¼ cup onion and blend until smooth. If you can spare the time, let this mixture culture for a couple hours. If not, don't worry about it. To the blender, add cauliflower, olive oil, celery, red onion, dill, garlic, ginger, jalapeño, Nama Shoyu, and lime zest, and blend until creamy. Spoon the mixture in equal portions into the romaine leaves (i.e., your spring roll wrappers) and sprinkle ¼ cup mint leaves and chopped burdock on top of the blended mixture in each leaf. Arrange decoratively on a platter and serve with Sweet & Sour Sauce.

FOR PASTA:

2 cups zucchini and/or squash

$1/2$ cup red bell pepper sliced into long, thin pasta-like strips

$1/2$ cup Marinated Onion Ringlets (for recipe see page 238)

$1/2$ cup diced tomato

$1/4$ cup Cured Eggplant, chopped (for recipe see page 237)

$1/4$ cup fresh basil, chopped

1 tablespoon fresh oregano, chopped

1 tablespoon fresh rosemary, de-stemmed and chopped

$1/4$ cup sun-dried tomatoes

$1/4$ cup Marinated Portobello (for recipe see page 238)

1 teaspoon minced jalapeño

1 teaspoon minced garlic

1 teaspoon minced ginger

$1/4$ cup lemon juice

FOR SAUCE:

$2/3$ cup RAW Pesto Sauce (for recipe see page 220)

$1/4$ cup olive oil

2 tablespoons Nama Shoyu or 1 teaspoon Celtic sea salt

$1/4$ cup sun-dried tomatoes

2 cups coconut water (from 1 to 2 coconuts) or other liquid

FOR GARNISH:

$1/4$ cup chopped scallions

$1/4$ cup green olives, pitted and chopped

Serves **2**

PESTO PASTA

With a potato peeler, shave zucchini and/or squash lengthwise into long, thin strips; when you've shaved all sides down to the center's seeds, slice the remaining portion into long strips. In a serving bowl combine the zucchini and/or squash strips, red bell pepper, Marinated Onion Ringlets, tomato, Cured Eggplant, basil, oregano, rosemary, sun-dried tomatoes, Marinated Portobello, jalapeño, garlic, ginger, and lemon juice. Mix and set aside.

In a blender combine the RAW Pesto Sauce, olive oil, Nama Shoyu or Celtic sea salt, sun-dried tomatoes, and coconut water or other liquid. Blend and pour over the vegetable pasta. Garnish with scallions and green olives. Serve immediately.

FOR PASTA:

2 cups zucchini and/or squash

$1/2$ cup red or yellow bell pepper sliced into long, thin pasta-like strips

$1/2$ cup Marinated Onion Ringlets (for recipe see page 238)

$1/4$ cup fresh tarragon, de-stemmed and chopped

2 cups Marinated Portobello (for recipe see page 238)

1 teaspoon minced jalapeño

1 teaspoon minced garlic

2 teaspoons minced ginger

1 tablespoon fresh-squeezed lemon juice

1 tablespoon white wine

$1/2$ cup minced shallots

FOR SAUCE:

1 recipe Mac Cream (for recipe see page 254)

Serves 2

THE ALFREDO SAUCE THAT GOES WITH THIS PASTA DISH SHOULD BE BLENDED *AFTER* EVERYTHING ELSE IS READY TO GO.

FETTUCCINE ALFREDO

With a vegetable peeler, shave zucchini and/or squash lengthwise into long, thin strips; when you've shaved all sides down to the soft and seedy center, slice the remaining portion into long strips. In a serving bowl combine zucchini and/or squash, bell pepper, Marinated Onion Ringlets, tarragon, Marinated Portobello, jalapeño, garlic, ginger, lemon juice, white wine, and shallots. Mix and set aside. Pour freshly prepared Mac Cream over the vegetable pasta and serve immediately.

FOR PASTA:

2 cups zucchini and/or squash

$^1/_2$ cup red or yellow bell pepper sliced into long,
  thin pasta-like strips

$^1/_2$ cup Marinated Onion Ringlets
  (for recipe see page 238)

$^1/_2$ cup diced tomato

$^1/_4$ cup fresh basil, chopped

2 tablespoons fresh oregano, chopped

1 tablespoon fresh rosemary, de-stemmed and chopped

$^1/_4$ cup sun-dried tomatoes (for a thicker sauce, add extra)

$^1/_3$ cup Marinated Portobello (for recipe see page 238)

1 teaspoon minced jalapeño

1 teaspoon minced garlic

1 teaspoon minced ginger

1 tablespoon lemon juice

$^1/_4$ cup minced shallots

Serves 2

FOR SAUCE:

1 recipe of Exquisite RAW Marinara Sauce
  (for recipe see page 219)

AND IF YOU WANT A GOOD LAUGH, SERVE THIS TO AN OLD-TIMER ITALIAN AND GET A SNAP SHOT OF THEIR EXPRESSION! Seriously go for it by making Meatballs out of the Meat Loaf recipe (minus the sauce) and adding them to this recipe.

PASTA MARINARA

With a vegetable peeler, shave zucchini and/or squash lengthwise into long, thin strips; when you've shaved all sides down to the soft and seedy center, slice the remaining portion into long strips. In a serving bowl combine zucchini and/or squash, bell pepper, Marinated Onion Ringlets, tomato, basil, oregano, rosemary, sun-dried tomatoes, Marinated Portobello, jalapeño, garlic, ginger, lemon juice, and shallots. Set aside. Make a fresh batch of Exquisite RAW Marinara Sauce and pour it over the vegetable pasta.

ARINARA

FOR PASTA:

2 cups zucchini and/or squash

1/2 cup red or yellow bell pepper sliced into long, thin pasta-like
   strips

1/2 cup Marinated Onion Ringlets (for recipe see page 238)

1/2 cup diced tomato

1/4 cup fresh basil, chopped

1/4 cup fresh cilantro, chopped

1/2 cup chopped mint

1/2 Marinated Portobello (for recipe see page 238)

1/4 cup chopped scallion

1/4 cup chopped shallots

1 tablespoon Curry Chutney (for recipe see page 238)

2/3 tablespoon minced galanga

1 tablespoon minced garlic

1 tablespoon minced ginger

2 teaspoons Thai chilies, minced

2 tablespoons fresh-squeezed lime juice

2 tablespoons chopped almonds

FOR SAUCE:

2 tablespoons lime leaves (kaffir lime), finely minced

1 tablespoon lemon grass, finely minced

2/3 cup Raw Ricotta Cheese (for recipe see page 255)
   or Mac Cream (for recipe see page 254)

1/4 cup olive oil

1/4 cup Nama Shoyu

1 1/2 cups coconut water (from 2 coconuts) or other liquid

1 teaspoon Thai chilies, chopped

1 tablespoon white wine

Serves 2 THAI PASTA

With a potato peeler, shave zucchini and/or squash lengthwise into
long, thin strips; when you've shaved all sides down to the soft and
seedy center, slice the remaining portion into long strips. In a serving
bowl combine zucchini and/or squash, bell peppers, Marinated Onion
Ringlets, tomato, basil, cilantro, mint, Marinated Portobello, scallions,
shallots, Curry Chutney, galanga, garlic, ginger, Thai chilies, and lime
juice. Mix and set aside. In a blender combine kaffir lime, lemon grass,
Raw Ricotta Cheese, olive oil, Nama Shoyu, coconut water or other liquid, and Thai chilies. Blend well and pour over pasta. Splash the wine
over the pasta, top with chopped almonds, and serve immediately.

Serves 2

LOTUS MANITOK

1 cup red bell pepper, julienne
1 cup carrots, julienne
$1/2$ cup zucchini, shaved into long strips with
 a vegetable peeler
$1/2$ cup red beets, julienne
$1/4$ cup chiogga beets, sliced
$1/2$ cup yams, sliced
$1/4$ cup walnuts, quartered
$1/4$ cup black Manitok rice, sprouted
 (for recipe see page 7)
$1/4$ cup chopped dill
$1/2$ cup apples, julienne
1 cup maple syrup
2 cups fresh-squeezed orange juice
$1/4$ cup fresh-squeezed lemon juice
$1/4$ cup olive oil
$1/4$ cup balsamic vinegar
$1/4$ cup Nama Shoyu
1 tablespoon minced ginger
2 $1/2$ teaspoons minced garlic
2 $1/2$ teaspoons minced jalapeño
1 tablespoon fresh cranberries
$1/4$ cup sunchokes, sliced
1 tablespoon grated lemon rind
1 tablespoon grated orange rind

Combine all the
above ingredients
in a serving bowl,
mix, and serve.

1 cup shiitake mushrooms, chopped
$\frac{1}{2}$ cup Nama Shoyu for soaking mushrooms
$\frac{1}{4}$ cup ginger, peeled paper thin with a vegetable peeler
$\frac{1}{4}$ cup apple cider vinegar for soaking ginger
1 cup daikon
$\frac{1}{2}$ cup zucchini
1 tablespoon apple cider vinegar
2 tablespoons Nama Shoyu
1 cup olive oil
$\frac{1}{3}$ cup fresh-squeezed orange juice
$\frac{1}{3}$ cup fresh-squeezed lemon juice
1 tablespoon white wine
1 cup bok choy, chopped
1 cup red bell pepper, diced
1 cup carrots, sliced into disks
1 cup chopped broccoli
$\frac{1}{2}$ cup chopped green onions
$\frac{1}{2}$ cup chopped shallots
$\frac{1}{2}$ cup red beets, julienne
$\frac{1}{2}$ cup yam, julienne
$\frac{1}{2}$ cup pepper cress, chopped
$\frac{1}{2}$ cup water chestnuts, peeled and chopped
$\frac{1}{4}$ cup chopped cashews
$\frac{1}{2}$ cup green beans
$\frac{1}{4}$ cup fresh parsley, chopped
$\frac{1}{4}$ cup purple cabbage, sliced thin
$\frac{1}{4}$ cup sprouted black or brown wild rice
 (for recipe see page 7)
1 tablespoon minced ginger
1 tablespoon minced garlic
1 teaspoon minced jalapeño

Serves 4

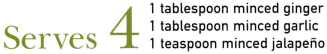

RAW STIR-FRY

Soak shiitake or other mushrooms in Nama Shoyu for 10 minutes to 1 day. Drain and set aside. Soak the thinly sliced ginger in apple cider vinegar for 1 hour to 1 year. Drain. With a potato peeler, shave daikon and zucchini lengthwise into long, thin strips; when you've shaved all sides down to the soft and seedy center, slice the remaining portion into long strips. In a serving bowl combine shiitake mushrooms and sliced ginger with the remaining ingredients. Mix and serve.

1 pound carrots (for 1 cup fresh carrot juice)
3 medium beets (for 1 cup fresh beet juice)
1 cucumber, peeled
2 medium tomatoes
1 cup red bell pepper, chopped
$1/4$ cup purple cabbage, sliced thin
1 cup sliced carrots
$1/2$ cup chopped shallots
$1/2$ cup red beets, julienne
$1/2$ cup yam, julienne
$1/2$ cup water chestnuts, peeled and chopped
$1/4$ cup fresh cilantro, chopped
$2/3$ cup black Manitok rice, sprouted
 (for recipe see page 7)
$1/2$ tablespoon minced ginger
$1/2$ tablespoon minced garlic
1 teaspoon minced jalapeño
$1/4$ cup Nama Shoyu
$1/2$ cup fresh-squeezed lemon juice
$1/2$ cup olive oil

Serves 2

MANITOK STEW

With a juicer, juice the carrots, beets, cucumber, and tomato. If you don't have a juicer, get the carrot and beet juice at a health food store and combine them in a blender with the peeled cucumber and tomato. Transfer the vegetable juice to a serving bowl and mix in the remaining ingredients. Serve immediately.

LIVE CHILI

$1/2$ pound carrots (for $1/2$ cup fresh carrot juice)
1 $1/2$ medium beets (for $1/2$ cup fresh beet juice)
$2/3$ cup sprouted black or other beans
  (for recipe see page 7)
1 full recipe of Barbeque Sauce
  (for recipe see page 216)
$1/2$ cup chopped red bell pepper
$1/2$ cup chopped fresh tomato
1 $1/2$ teaspoons minced garlic
1 teaspoon minced jalapeño
1 teaspoon minced ginger
$1/4$ cup chopped shallots
$1/4$ cup red wine
$1/4$ cup fresh parsley, chopped
1 recipe Mocksarella Cheese
  (optional; for recipe see page 260)

In a juicer, juice the carrots and beets until you have $1/2$ cup juice of each (or purchase juice from a health food deli). In a serving bowl, combine the juices with the remaining ingredients, mix and serve. If you have a little extra time, you can throw it in the dehydrator for an hour at 100°F and, dare I say, eat it warm. For a melted cheese effect, place a slice of Mocksarella on top of each serving before dehydrating.

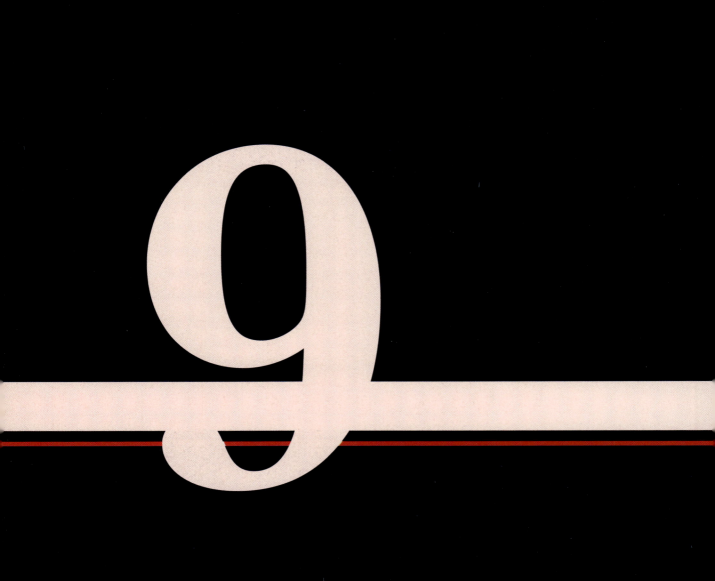

DESSERTS

OATMEA

Makes **12** cookies

OATMEAL COOKIES

2 cups oat groats

$^3/_4$ cup dates

$^1/_2$ cup dried raisins, chopped

$^1/_2$ cup raw almonds, coarsely chopped

2 or 3 apples, coarsely grated
(optional; use only if you prefer a chewier, heavier cookie)

$^1/_2$ cup raw cashews

Place oat groats in a food processor and grind until fine. If you don't have a food processor, use a blender and add a little maple syrup to help the dough turn over. Transfer the groats to a mixing bowl and add the dates, raisins, almonds, and apple (optional) and mix the batter well. Set aside. In a coffee grinder grind the cashews until they resemble a silky flour. On a mesh dehydrator sheet shape the batter into the desired cookie shapes, using the cashew flour for easier handling of the batter. Keep in mind that the thicker you shape the cookies, the longer they take to dehydrate. Dehydrate the cookies at 90°F until they reach your preferred texture, around 12 hours. They don't need to be crunchy all the way through.

CRUNCHY FLAX SEED COOKIES

THIS IS A VERY VERSATILE RECIPE; YOU CAN TRY MAKING THEM WITH WHOLE OR FINELY GROUND FLAX SEEDS, TOO.

Makes 12 cookies

2 cups flax seeds
1 cup maple syrup
4 cups coarsely pureed apples
   (preferably Fuji or Braeburn)
$^1/_2$ cup chopped raw walnuts (optional)
dash of cinnamon

Put flax seeds, $^1/_2$ cup at a time, in coffee grinder or food processor and coarsely grind. If you don't have a food processor, use a blender. Transfer the ground flax seeds into a mixing bowl, add the remaining ingredients and mix thoroughly. Spoon the flax seed dough into desired cookie shapes on a mesh dehydrator sheet and dehydrate at 90°F for 12 hours, or until crisp on the outside and gooey on the inside.

2 ½ cups freshly scraped coconut meat, chopped
2 cups maple syrup
1 teaspoon vanilla extract
1 cup raw cashew butter
1 cup raw carob powder
⅓ cup chopped raw pecans
⅓ cup chopped raw cashews
⅓ cup chopped raw macadamia nuts

JUL'S CASHEW BUTTER FUDGE COOKIES

NO DESSERT ON THE PLANET EVEN COMES CLOSE!

Makes 12 cookies

In a food processor puree the coconut meat, maple syrup, and vanilla extract until it's creamy. If you don't have a food processor, use a blender and add a little orange juice to help the dough turn over. Add the cashew butter and carob and puree.

Form the pureed mixture into cookie shapes on a lightly oiled mesh dehydrator sheet and dehydrate at 90°F for 18 hours.

Press the pecans, cashews and macadamia nuts into each cookie. Don't be surprised if they never make it the entire dehydrating time; in my kitchen after 7 hours, we can't take it anymore and eat them raw.

CASHEW BUTTER COOKIES

Follow the Jul's Cashew Butter Fudge Cookies recipe, but omit the carob.

Makes 12 cookies

3 cups oats
2 cups pitted dates
filtered water for soaking oats and dates
$^1/_4$ cup maple syrup or honey
1 cup raw pecans
1 teaspoon mace
2 cups raw walnuts and almonds, coarsely chopped

Soak the oats and dates in separate containers with enough water to cover for 2 hours. Drain. In a blender combine oats and maple syrup or honey and blend until creamy. Spoon blender contents, about $^1/_8$ inch thick, onto a solid dehydrator sheet and dehydrate until crispy, about 6 hours. Transfer oat crust onto a pie plate. Set aside.

In a food processor (or Champion juicer), homogenize dates and pecans and spread a 1-inch layer of the mixture over the oat crust. Evenly sprinkle one third of the walnuts, almonds, and a pinch of mace over date-nut paste. Repeat the layering process until you've used all the date-nut paste, nuts, and mace; it makes up to three layers.

Serves 8

BAKLAVA

²/₃ cup walnuts
2 cups water
1 tablespoon vanilla extract (optional)
²/₃ cup maple syrup

Serves 2

Soak the walnuts in enough water to cover for 2 hours. Drain. Liquefy all the ingredients in a blender. For flavor variations, when making the shake you can add a handful of strawberries, mango, raspberries, a dash of grated orange or lemon rind, or a scoop of carob powder to create delectable flavors!

Pour the liquid into ice cube trays and freeze. Allow the cubes to thaw for 5 minutes then puree them in a food processor or blender. If you have a Champion, push the cubes through and they transform into thick, rich ice cream! Spoon the frozen cream into a glass and add your favorite toppings. I use Swirled Bubble Gum, Buckwheaties, crushed frozen raspberries, chocolate mint, and a drizzle of Black Tar.

MILK SHAKE

Serves 4

**CHOCOLATE FLAVORED PUDDING
THAT'S ACTUALLY GOOD FOR YOU!**

EZ PUDDING

1 cup maple syrup or 1 $\frac{1}{2}$ cups dates
2 medium avocados
$\frac{1}{2}$ cup carob powder

Throw the ingredients into a blender and blend well. Stop the blender and scrape the sides to be sure all the ingredients mix thoroughly. Blend until fluffy.

If you use dates, rather than maple syrup, add a little orange juice to the blender or soak the dates in orange juice before using.

CASHE

CASHEW GELATO

2 cups raw cashew butter
1 $1/2$ cups maple syrup
$2/3$ cup almonds, coarsely chopped

In a bowl mix the cashew butter and maple syrup.
Fold in chopped almonds. Spoon the mixture into
individual serving bowls and freeze. Throw in $1/2$
cup raw carob powder for a chocolate variation!
Serve frozen.

Serves 2

MASH IT

1 plantain or banana
$1/_2$ cup of your favorite berries
$1/_2$ cup dates
1 tablespoon raw carob powder
$1/_4$ cup any type of nut butter (optional)

Serves 2

Mash and munch.

A BOWL, A FORK, AND YOU'VE GOT AN AMAZING DESSERT!

MAS

ROBBIN'S ICE CREAM

THIS RECIPE SERVES FOUR, BUT YOU MAY WANT TO QUADRUPLE IT—YOU'LL END UP EATING THE WHOLE THING YOURSELF!

IT

1 cup frozen mango (dice and freeze your own!)
2 cups fresh-squeezed orange juice
1 cup raw cashews
1 cup banana, frozen
2 cups soft or soaked dates

Blend and eat (or if you can wait, chill in the freezer for around 20 minutes).

Serves 10
RAW TORTE

FOR FILLING:
5 cups of dates, pitted
coconut water for soaking the dates
2 cups coconut meat (if fresh, diced)
1 cup Buckwheaties (optional, but recommended
since they make the torte taste like a
Crunch bar; for recipe see page 231)
4 cups raw carob powder
4 cups raw almond, raw cashew,
or raw hazelnut butter
3 tablespoons vanilla extract (optional)
2 cups maple syrup
2 cups Whipped Cream (for recipe see page 253)

FOR CRUST:
1 cup Buckwheaties (for recipe see page 231)
1 cup maple syrup
1 cup raw almonds
1 $\frac{1}{4}$ cups raw walnuts
1 date, pitted
1 tablespoon raw nut butter

FOR GARNISH (OPTIONAL):
1 tablespoon pomegranate seeds
1 tablespoon raspberries
1 tablespoon sliced strawberries
1 tablespoon sprouted Quinoa
(for recipe see page 7)
1 tablespoon chocolate mint
1 tablespoon Black Tar (for recipe see page 183)
1 tablespoon edible flower petals

WHILE YOU MAY USE ANY TYPE OF NUT BUTTER IN THIS RECIPE, I'VE FOUND CASHEW BUTTER TASTES BEST. YOU CAN ALSO SUBSTITUTE FAST CAKE CRUST FOR THE CRUST DESCRIBED BELOW (FOR RECIPE SEE PAGE 184).

Unless you're using very soft, creamy dates, soak the dates in coconut water for 1 or 2 hours prior to using them. Drain the dates and set them aside, saving the coconut water for future use. Mince the coconut meat by hand or in a food processor one cup at a time, until each chunk is a bit larger than a chocolate chip. In a large mixing bowl, combine the coconut meat, Buckwheaties (optional), and carob and mix until the coconut and Buckwheaties are well-coated with carob. There should still be at least $\frac{1}{2}$ cup of carob in the bottom of the bowl after all coconut meat and Buckwheaties are coated. Set aside. In a food processor puree the dates and maple syrup. Add the date puree, nut butter, and vanilla extract (optional) to the carob coconut mixture. Mix well.

Make the crust. In a food processor puree the Buckwheaties, maple syrup, almonds, walnuts, date, and nut butter. Oil a 9-inch round pie plate with olive oil and press the pureed crust into it. The crust should be thin. Spoon the torte filling into the crust and cover it with the Whipped Cream. Put the torte into the freezer for 2 hours. It will not freeze, but should be served chilled and garnished with pomegranates, raspberries, sliced strawberries, sprouted Quinoa, chocolate mint, a drizzle of Black Tar, and edible flowers. Store leftovers (yeah right!) in the freezer.

NUTTY DREAMS

IF YOU DON'T HAVE A
DREAM, HOW CAN YOU HAVE
A DREAM COME TRUE?

Makes 12

1 cup raw almond
 or raw cashew butter
1 cup maple syrup
$1/2$ cup raw walnuts coarsely chopped
$1/2$ cup raw almonds coarsely chopped
2 tablespoons Buckwheaties
 (for recipe see page 231)
$1/4$ cup raw carob powder

Combine all the ingredients in a
bowl and mix well. Form the mixture into
bite-size balls and serve.

Serves 2

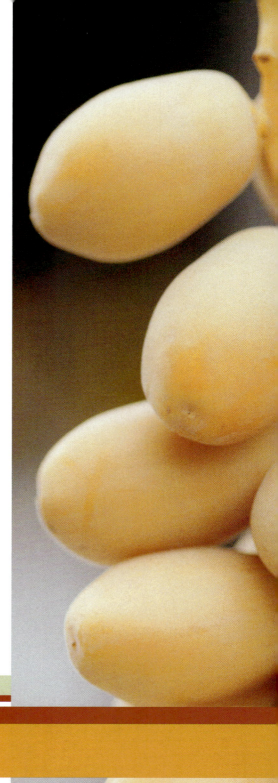

$^1/_2$ cup avocado
$^2/_3$ cup dates
$^1/_3$ cup raw carob powder
$^1/_4$ cup Black Tar
$^1/_4$ cup raw cashew or almond butter

In a blender (or food processor) puree the avocado, dates, carob powder, Black Tar, and cashew or almond butter. Spoon the mousse into goblets and garnish with your favorite toppings. I use Buckwheaties, crushed frozen raspberries and chocolate mint.

CAROB MOUSSE

Serves 2

1 cup dates
$^1/_2$ cup dates
2 teaspoons vanilla extract
 (optional)

In a blender or food processor, puree the dates, and
vanilla extract (optional).
Spoon the mousse into goblets and garnish with your
favorite toppings. I throw on
a few crushed frozen raspberries and chocolate mint.

VANILLA MOUSSE

DURIAN, MANGO, MULBERRY, MAPLE SYRUP (OR DATE) AVO MOUSSE

$^1/_4$ cup durian (optional)
1 cup freshly frozen mango
 (that means *you* chop and freeze it)
$^1/_2$ cup mulberries or other berry
1 cup avocado
$^2/_3$ cup maple syrup

Blend until fluffy and serve.

Serves 2

FOR CAKE:

2 cups dates, pitted and soaked
2 pounds carrots (for 2 cups carrot pulp)
2 cups meat from a young coconut, minced
$1/4$ cup ginger
1 $1/2$ cups fresh carrot juice
$3/4$ cup organic raisins,
  soaked a few minutes and drained
2 cups raw walnuts, coarsely chopped
1 $1/2$ teaspoons cinnamon
$1/2$ teaspoon ground cardamon
1 teaspoon nutmeg
3 cups Whipped Cream (for recipe see page 253)
1 recipe Fast Cake Crust (for recipe see page 184)

Serves 2

CARROT CAKE

ARE YOU READY TO MAKE THE MOISTEST, MOST FLAVORFUL, FRESHEST, NO-BAKE, 15-MINUTE CARROT CAKE YOU'VE EVER TASTED?

FOR ORANGE GLAZE:

1 cup fresh-squeezed orange juice
1 tablespoon grated orange rind
1 tablespoon grated lemon rind
$1/2$ cup dates
2 tablespoons fresh-squeezed lemon juice
2 tablespoons cashew butter

Unless you're using very soft, creamy dates you'll need to soak the dates in water for 1 or 2 hours prior to using. Drain and set aside. With a juicer, juice the carrots until you have 2 cups carrot pulp and 1 $1/2$ cups carrot juice. If you don't have a juicer, you can buy the pulp and juice at a health food store. In a blender combine the coconut, soaked dates, ginger, and enough carrot juice to get it to blend. Transfer the blender contents to a mixing bowl and mix in the carrot pulp, raisins, walnuts, cinnamon, cardamon, and nutmeg; this is your carrot cake.

Press the carrot cake into a pie plate covered with Fast Cake Crust and frost it with the Whipped Cream; it should be about a quarter of the height of the cake. Make the Orange Glaze by combining in a blender the orange juice, orange and lemon rinds, dates, lemon juice, and cashew butter and blending well. Drizzle the carrot cake with Orange Glaze and serve.

ROMANOFF

Serves 2
STRAWBERRY ROMANOFF

1 ¹/₂ cups Whipped Cream (for recipe see page 253)
1 cup sliced strawberries
¹/₂ cup other berries (optional)
2 tablespoons dates
1 tablespoon chocolate mint

In a serving bowl combine the Whipped Cream and berries and dates and mix well. Garnish with chocolate mint. Serve.

FOR DATE/FIG CAKE:

$^1/_2$ cup dates

$^1/_2$ cup dried figs

filtered water for soaking dates and figs

$^1/_2$ cup maple syrup

$^1/_2$ tablespoon vanilla extract

1 $^1/_2$ tablespoons raw carob powder

FOR RASPBERRY CREAM:

$^1/_2$ cup raw walnuts

$^1/_2$ cup frozen raspberries

$^1/_2$ cup maple syrup

1 tablespoon vanilla extract (optional)

Serves 2

For garnish (optional):

1 tablespoon pomegranate seeds

1 tablespoon raspberries

1 tablespoon sliced strawberries

1 tablespoon sprouted Quinoa
 (see page 7)

1 tablespoon chocolate mint

1 tablespoon Black Tar (for recipe see page 183)

1 tablespoon edible flowers

RASPBERRY TIRAMISU

YOU CAN EAT 2 OR 3 PIECES FOR DESSERT WITHOUT ONE OUNCE OF GUILT!

Soak dates and dried figs in water for two hours; drain. Puree the dates, figs, maple syrup, vanilla extract, and raw carob powder in a blender or food processor. If you have a Champion juicer, use it instead. Divide the date mixture in half and form one of the halves into a 4-inch-diameter circular mini cake on a dessert plate. Shape the other half the same way on another dessert plate. Set aside.

In a blender blend the walnuts, frozen raspberries, maple syrup, and vanilla extract until creamy. Spoon the Raspberry Cream evenly onto each date/fig cake. Sprinkle the top with a garnish of pomegranate seeds, raspberries, sliced strawberries, sprouted Quinoa, chocolate mint, a drizzle of Black Tar, and edible flowers. Serve immediately.

BLACK TAR

Makes 4 cups

3 cups maple syrup
$2/3$ cup olive oil
2 tablespoons vanilla extract (optional)
1 cup raw carob powder

Combine the above ingredients in a blender. Blend well and enjoy! Keeps indefinitely.

FAKE CAKE CRUST
Makes enough for 1 9-inch pie crust

YOU COULD LIVE ON THIS STUFF!

2 cups raw almonds
2 cups dates

On a cutting board chop the almonds and
dates thoroughly. Knead the nuts and dates
together and then press into a pie plate.
You can have dessert for breakfast, lunch,
and dinner and still be eating better than
anyone else on the planet!

10

DRINKS & SMOOTHIES

Serves **2**

So chocolatey, you'll get that amorous feeling you used to get only from chocolate!

CAROBANA SMOOTHIE

1 cup coconut water (from one coconut)
1 cup frozen banana
1 cup frozen berries or other sweet fruit
$^1/_2$ cup dates
5 tablespoons raw carob powder
$^1/_2$ cup young coconut flesh, chopped

Follow the Smoothie Preparation Guidelines below.

THAW FROZEN FRUIT FOR FIVE MINUTES. USE A LARGE KNIFE TO CHOP THE PARTIALLY-THAWED FRUIT INTO SMALL CHUNKS, AND IN A BLENDER BLEND WITH THE RECIPE'S REMAINING INGREDIENTS. IF THE CONTENTS WON'T BLEND, USE THE AID OF A RUBBER SCRAPER WHILE THE BLENDER IS RUNNING, BUT DON'T GET IT NEAR THE BLADES. YOU CAN ALSO TURN OFF THE BLENDER, PUSH THE CONTENTS DOWN TOWARD THE BLADES, START IT BACK UP AGAIN, AND BLEND UNTIL THICK AND CREAMY. DRINK IMMEDIATELY.

Serves 4

SANGRIA

2 bottles fine red or white wine
$^1/_2$ cup diced apples
$^1/_2$ cup diced mandarin or naval oranges
$^1/_2$ cup diced strawberries
$^1/_2$ cup diced pineapple
$^1/_2$ cup diced peaches
$^1/_2$ cup diced plums
$^1/_2$ cup diced apricots
$^1/_2$ cup diced bananas
$^1/_2$ cup other chopped berries

Pour bottles of fine red or white wine into
a glass container and add all of the fruit.
Let the sangria chill for two hours in
the refrigerator.

Serves 4

TEA #1

4 cups Rejuvelac (for recipe see page 194) or filtered water
$1/_2$ cup diced apples
$1/_2$ cup fresh mint, chopped
$1/_2$ cup unpeeled oranges, diced
1 tablespoon minced ginger
dried hibiscus flowers to taste

Combine all ingredients in a pitcher. Place in the hot sun
for one hour or soak indoors for a maximum of three
hours, then refrigerate.

TEA

TEA #2

4 cups Rejuvelac (for recipe see page 194) or
   filtered water
$^1/_2$ cup apple, diced
$^1/_2$ cup fresh mint, chopped
$^1/_2$ cup unpeeled orange, diced
1 tablespoon minced ginger
$^1/_2$ cup mint or fresh cilantro
$^1/_2$ cup any other herbs
   (rosemary, fresh thyme, sage, etc.)
hibiscus flowers to taste

Combine all ingredients in a pitcher. Place
in hot sun for six hours or soak indoors for
a maximum of 18 hours, then refrigerate.

I CALLED THIS "APPLE BLASTER" IN
MY RESTAURANT AND WE SOLD 1 A MONTH.
I CHANGED THE NAME TO "BLOOD" AND
NOW WE SELL 45 A DAY. SO, BLOOD IT IS.

BLOOD

Serves 4

2 pounds apples
1 piece ginger
  (about 2 tablespoons, unpeeled)
$^1/_2$ cup beet
$^1/_4$ cup fresh-squeezed lime juice

With a juicer juice all the ingredients, combine
them in a pitcher and allow the juice to chill.
Drink when cool.

2 cups sprouted wheat berries
 (for recipe see page 7)
3 cups filtered water

Soak the sprouted berries in the water for 9 hours, stirring once every hour or so to activate fermentation. If it doesn't ferment, discard it and try again.

Drain the water into a container and keep the wheat berries. The drained water is your Rejuvelac. Let the wheat berries breathe for a few hours, then use them again and again to make more Rejuvelac; each time it's stronger and better.

Strain the mixture and store in refrigerator. When refrigerated Rejuvelac lasts two weeks.

Serves 12 Makes three cups

A MAPLE-SYRUP-FLAVORED DRINK WITH A LEMONY ZING.

REJUVELAC

MANGO COCKTAIL

1 medium beet
  (for $1/4$ cup fresh beet juice)
1 cup frozen mango
1 $1/2$ cups Rejuvelac
  (for recipe see page 194)
  or liquid of your choice
2 tablespoons fresh-squeezed lime juice
2 tablespoons maple syrup
$1/2$ lime, for twists

In a juicer, juice the beet to produce
$1/4$ cup beet juice or purchase the juice
from a health food store. In a blender
combine the frozen mango, Rejuvelac,
lime juice, maple syrup, and beet juice.
Blend and serve with a twist of lime.
Throw in some white wine
or champagne if you wish.

Serves 2

MANGO COCKTA

1 medium beet (for $1/4$ cup fresh beet juice)
1 $1/2$ cups Rejuvelac
  (for recipe see page 194) or other liquid
$1/4$ cup fresh-squeezed lemon juice
$1/4$ cup fresh-squeezed lime juice
$1/4$ cup frozen pineapple, diced
$1/4$ cup maple syrup
$1/2$ lime
2 pineapple wedges, optional

Serves 2
LEMONADE

In a juicer, juice the beet to produce $1/4$ cup beet juice or buy it from a health food store. In a blender combine the Rejuvelac, lemon juice, lime juice, frozen pineapple, maple syrup, and beet juice. Blend and serve with a twist of lime and a pineapple wedge.

Serves 2

GINGER COCKTAIL

1 ¹/₂ cups Rejuvelac
  (for recipe see page 194) or filtered water
2 tablespoons maple syrup
2 tablespoons minced ginger
a handful of your favorite frozen berries
¹/₄ lime

In a blender combine the Rejuvelac, maple syrup,
and ginger. Blend and serve over "berry ice cubes"
(frozen berries) with a twist of lime.

CALL IT ESPRESSO FOR NATURALISTS. SERVE IT IN A SHOT GLASS AND TOSS IT BACK IN ONE GULP AND YOU'LL KNOW WHAT I MEAN.

FIREWATER

FIREWATER

FIREWATER

4 cups filtered water
1 tablespoon hottest hot peppers you can get,
  chopped (I recommend habanero chilis)
lemon, unpeeled and quartered
$1/2$ lime, unpeeled and quartered
1 orange, unpeeled and quartered
$1/2$ cup fresh mint, chopped
1 $1/2$ teaspoons minced ginger
1 medium beet, chopped

In a gallon glass jar combine all the above ingredients. Secure with a tight lid and set the jar in the sun for 20 hours. If it's winter, let it sit over night. Shake it up, then strain the liquid into a pitcher and refrigerate it. Makes 16 big shots.

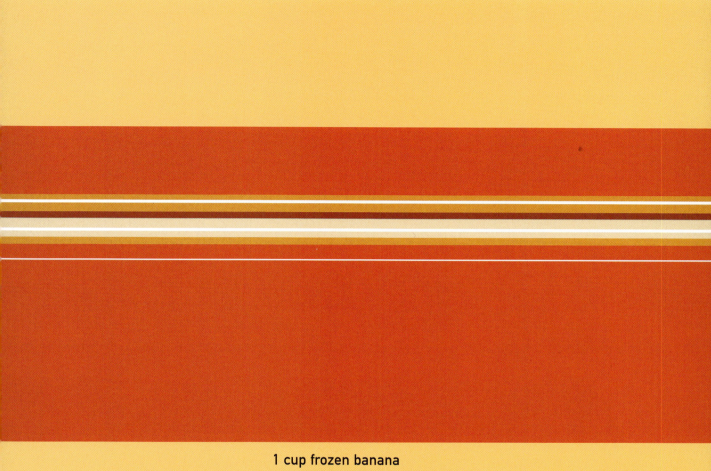

1 cup frozen banana
1 cup frozen berries or other sweet fruit
$^1/_2$ cup maple syrup
1 tablespoon Chai Chutney (for recipe see page 229)

Follow the Smoothie Preparation Guidelines on page 189.

CHAI SMOOTHIE

Serves 1

r o o t B a b y

1 pound carrots
1 tablespoon ginger, unpeeled
$1/2$ cup beets, chopped
$1/4$ medium lime
$1/4$ cup pomegranate seeds
1 cup apple, chopped

CARROT BABY

UNLESS YOU BUY FRESH-SQUEEZED JUICE, IT IS *ALWAYS* COOKED TO PRESERVE "FRESHNESS." THINK ABOUT IT!

With a juicer, juice the above ingredients
and combine them in a container.

Serves 2

Serves 2

SUNSHINE RAIN

$^1/_2$ cup frozen cantaloupe
$^1/_2$ cup fresh nectarines, peeled
$^1/_2$ cup frozen peaches, chopped
$^1/_2$ cup frozen mango, chopped
$^1/_2$ cup maple syrup or honey
1 teaspoon cinnamon
$^1/_2$ cup fresh-squeezed orange juice

Follow the Smoothie Preparation
Guidelines on page 189.

BLU

Blue Green Smoothie

1 cup frozen banana
1 cup frozen berries or other sweet fruit
$^1/_2$ cup maple syrup
1 tablespoon Hawaiian spiriolina
1 shot wheat grass juice
1 teaspoon blue green algae powder

Follow the Smoothie Preparation
Guidelines on page 189.

Serves 2

Serves 2

1 cup avocado
1 cup coconut water (from one coconut) or
   fresh-squeezed orange juice
$^1/_2$ cup maple syrup
$^1/_4$ cup raw carob powder
$^1/_2$ cup young coconut flesh, chopped

Put in blender and blend well.

CAROB
SMOOTHIE

CASHEW BUTTER SMOOTHIE

Serves 2

1 cup frozen bananas
1 cup frozen berries or other sweet fruit
$1/2$ cup maple syrup
2 tablespoons cashew butter

Follow the Smoothie Preparation
Guidelines on page 189.

CARIBBEAN SMOOTHIE

Serves 2

DRINK IT, THEN GO JUMP IN THE OCEAN!

$1/2$ cup coconut water (from one coconut)

$1/2$ cup frozen banana

$1/2$ cup frozen berries or other sweet fruit

$1/2$ cup maple syrup

$1/4$ cup frozen mango

$1/4$ cup frozen pineapple, chopped

$1/4$ cup frozen papaya

$1/4$ cup young coconut flesh, chopped

Follow the Smoothie Preparation Guidelines on page 189.

REFLAX SMOOTHIE

$1/3$ cup flax seeds
$1/3$ cup almonds
3 cups fresh-squeezed orange juice
$1/2$ cup young coconut meat, chopped, optional
$1/2$ cup dates, pitted, optional
$1/2$ cup frozen fruit, optional

In a coffee grinder or food processor grind the flax seeds and almonds. Transfer them to a blender, add orange juice and selected optional ingredients, blend, and serve.

Serves 2

MANGO SMOOTHIE

2 cups frozen mango
$1/2$ cup maple syrup

Follow the Smoothie Preparation Guidelines on page 189.

BERRY SMOOTHIE

1 cup frozen banana
$^1/_2$ cup frozen strawberries
$^1/_2$ cup frozen raspberries
$^1/_2$ cup frozen blackberries
$^1/_2$ cup maple syrup

Follow the Smoothie Preparation
Guidelines on page 189.

DRESSINGS, SAUCES, MARINADES & CONDIMENTS

Serves 4

RAW RESTAURANT'S
HOUSE DRESSING

**IT'S SO GOOD PEOPLE ORDER IT
AS A SOUP IN MY RESTAURANT.**

$^1/_2$ cup fresh-squeezed lemon juice
1 $^1/_2$ cups olive oil
2 tablespoons minced ginger
$^1/_3$ cup minced garlic
3 tablespoons Nama Shoyu

Place all the ingredients in blender
and blend until creamy and smooth, about 2
minutes. This dressing keeps about 5 days in
the refrigerator.

Dressing for 4 main course salads.

Serves 4
PAPAYA DRESSING

THIS RECIPE CAN DOUBLE AS A DIPPING SAUCE FOR FRENCH FRIES.

1 ripe papaya (around one cup) peeled and seeded
1 $^1/_2$ cups fresh-squeezed orange juice
$^1/_4$ cup fresh-squeezed lime juice

Blend and serve.

Makes enough for 4 side salads.

THIS RECIPE CAN ALSO DOUBLE AS A DIPPING SAUCE FOR FRENCH FRIES.

1 tablespoon ginger, unpeeled and minced
1 ripe mango
$1/2$ cup coconut water or Rejuvelac

Combine the ingredients in a blender and blend well. This dressing keeps for 3 days when refrigerated.

Serves 4 Makes enough for 4 salads.

MANGO-GIN DRESSING

Serves 4

SESAME SEED DRESSING

1 cup sesame seeds
2 cups filtered water for soaking sesame seeds
$1/2$ cup Rejuvelac or filtered water
$1/2$ cup fresh parsley, chopped
1 tablespoon minced garlic
1 tablespoon fresh dill, de-stemmed and chopped
1 tablespoon fresh oregano leaves, chopped
1 tablespoon fresh basil leaves, chopped
$1/4$ cup olive oil
$1/3$ cup fresh-squeezed lemon juice
$1/4$ cup Nama Shoyu or 1 $1/2$ teaspoons Celtic sea salt

Soak sesame seeds in water for 2 hours. Drain. In a blender combine seeds and all other ingredients listed above. Blend until creamy. This dressing keeps for 3 days when refrigerated.

Makes enough for 4 salads.

Serves **12**

BARBEQUE SAUCE
(A.K.A. CHILI SAUCE)

1 cup fresh tomatoes, chopped

$^1/_4$ cup chopped onion

$^1/_2$ cup sun-dried tomatoes, chopped

$^1/_2$ teaspoon minced garlic

$^3/_4$ teaspoon minced jalapeño

4 fresh basil leaves

$^1/_2$ cup Mèdjool dates, pitted

olive oil or fresh tomato juice for blending

$^1/_4$ cup Nama Shoyu or 1 teaspoon Celtic
   sea salt

1 tablespoon olive oil

Combine the above ingredients in a food processor or a blending jar and blend. Add a little tomato juice or olive oil if the sauce is too thick to blend. Stir in Nama Shoyu or Celtic sea salt, and olive oil. Keeps for 2 days in the refrigerator.

Makes 2 $^1/_2$ cups.

I DON'T USE PEANUTS IN MY PEANUT SAUCE
because raw organic peanuts don't taste very good and most non-organic peanut farmers grow pesticide-sprayed cotton in between their peanut plants.

Serves 2
PEANUT SAUCE

$^1/_2$ cup raw cashew butter
$^1/_4$ cup dates
$^1/_2$ cup fresh-squeezed orange juice
$^1/_4$ cup Nama Shoyu
$^1/_4$ cup raw almonds, chopped

Combine cashew butter, dates, orange juice, and Nama Shoyu in a blender and blend until creamy. Fold in almonds and serve. Keeps for 2 days in the refrigerator.

Makes 2 $^3/_4$ cups.

Serves 2

**I USE THIS TANGY SAUCE TO TOP
RAW SPRING ROLLS; IT GOES GREAT
WITH ANY SUSHI RECIPE, TOO!**

$1/_4$ cup dates
2 teaspoons mustard
1 teaspoon apple cider vinegar
2 tablespoons olive oil
1 tablespoon minced ginger
2 tablespoons fresh-squeezed orange juice
$1/_4$ cup fresh-squeezed lemon juice
2 tablespoons Nama Shoyu

Combine all the ingredients in a
mixing bowl. Whisk and serve. Keeps
for 2 days in the refrigerator.

Makes 1 cup.

SWEET & SOUR SAUCE

½ cup dried pineapple or mango (optional)
½ cup strawberries
2 cups chopped tomatoes,
  preferably cherry or heirloom
1 teaspoon minced ginger
2 tablespoons minced garlic
1 teaspoon minced jalapeño
⅓ cup fresh basil leaves, chopped and packed
⅓ cup red bell pepper, minced
¼ cup fresh oregano leaves,
  de-stemmed and chopped
¼ cup Nama Shoyu
  or 1 ½ teaspoons Celtic sea salt
1 cup olive oil
½ cup sun-dried tomatoes, chopped
2 green olives, pitted
¼ cup red wine
¼ cup shallots

EXQUISITE RAW MARINARA SAUCE

Serves 2

Place all ingredients into blender and blend until creamy, about 1 or 2 minutes. This sauce thickens about 2 or 3 minutes after blending; do not blend the sauce until just before you're ready to eat use it.

Serves 2
RAW PESTO SAUCE

THIS SAUCE SHOULD TASTE A LITTLE TOO
SALTY BECAUSE I USE IT IN VARIOUS
RECIPES WHERE THE PESTO MUST CARRY
THE SALT FOR THE ENTIRE DISH.

$1/3$ cup garlic
2 cups pine nuts
2 cups fresh basil leaves, packed
2 cups raw walnuts
$1/3$ cup black miso

In a food processor or blender, homogenize garlic
and basil leaves. Ground nuts into powder then add.
Stir in black miso. If you have a Green Power, use it;
it works best. Keeps for 5 days in the refrigerator.

Makes 3 cups.

CILANTRO PESTO

2 cups fresh cilantro, chopped and packed
$2/3$ cup walnuts
$2/3$ cup fresh-squeezed lime juice
1 $1/2$ teaspoons Celtic sea salt or $1/4$ cup Nama Shoyu
$1/2$ cup spinach, optional
1 tablespoon garlic
1 tablespoon minced ginger
$1/4$ teaspoon habanero chili or 2 teaspoons jalapeño, minced
$1/2$ cup olive oil

In a blender, blend all above ingredients into a green cream, using a scraper to help turn it over.

Makes approximately 4 cups.

GRAV

SERVE THIS OVER MASHED POTATOES ON A COLD WINTER NIGHT.

GRAVY

$^1/_4$ cup miso
1 tablespoon red wine
$^1/_2$ cup chopped onion
1 minced shallot
1 tablespoon minced garlic
$^1/_4$ cup fresh-squeezed orange juice
   or carrot juice
$^1/_3$ cup olive oil
1 tablespoon dates
1 teaspoon jalapeño
1 tablespoon Nama Shoyu
1 tablespoon minced ginger
1 teaspoon apple cider vinegar
$^1/_2$ teaspoon sesame seed oil

Combine all ingredients in a blender and blend until creamy.

Makes around 3 cups of Gravy.

I TRY TO AVOID USING WATER WHEN RAWING.

When I need to add liquid to a savory recipe (especially when blending grains and a little moisture is needed to help them turn over), I often use this recipe. If I need water for a sweet recipe I use fresh-squeezed orange juice, or blended melon or other juicy fruits.

2 cucumbers, peeled
$1/2$ cup fresh-squeezed lemon juice
$1/2$ tomato (optional)

Blend all the ingredients in a blender and voilà, you've got pure, crisp-flavored water.

Makes around 5 cups Water.

WATER

SEAWEED WATER

1 cup of dried (not roasted) seaweed
3 cups filtered water

Soak seaweed in water. Follow directions on dried seaweed package for amount of time to soak. Drain the water (saving it) and eat the seaweed. Seaweed Water keeps for 2 days in the refrigerator.

Makes 3 cups.

WATEI

CHUTNE

JULIANO'S SPICE CHUTNEY

I PRE-MIX THIS CHUTNEY SO IT'S READILY AVAILABLE WHENEVER I NEED IT.

For the ultimate chutney, order the spices from Foods of India
121 Lexington Avenue, New York, NY 10016
(212)683-4419 phone and (212)251-0946 fax.

$1/4$ cup sun-dried lime
$1/4$ cup Mexican Spice Chutney
  (for recipe see below)
$1/4$ cup paprika
$1/4$ cup turmeric
$1/4$ cup sumac
$1/4$ cup yellow (or golden) curry
$1/2$ teaspoon nutmeg
$1/4$ cup cinnamon
$1/4$ cup corriander

Grind the sun-dried lime in a coffee grinder.
Combine with other ingredients and store
the mix in a tightly sealed jar.
Makes 2 cups.

MEXICAN SPICE CHUTNEY

THIS IS ANOTHER SPICE COMBO I MIX IN ADVANCE AND KEEP ON HAND.

$1/2$ cup black cumin
$1/2$ cup sun-dried lime

Grind the sun-dried lime in a coffee grinder.
Mix in spice.
Store the mix in a tightly sealed jar.
Makes about $3/4$ cup.

CUR

**THE THIRD IN MY TRIO OF
ESSENTIAL SPICE CHUTNEYS.**

$1/2$ cup yellow (or golden) curry
$1/2$ cup sun-dried lime

Grind the sun-dried lime in a coffee grinder.
Mix in spice. Store the mix in a tightly sealed jar.
Makes about $3/4$ cup.

CURRY CHUTNEY

2 cups of dates in 2 cups of water
2 tablespoons raw carob powder
1 tablespoon cinnamon
1 teaspoon nutmeg
$1/_4$ cup minced ginger
$1/_2$ cup olive oil
1 tablespoon vanilla extract optional

Blend the above ingredients well. Store in a jar and keep it in the refrigerator.
Makes about 2 $3/_4$ cups.

CHAI SPICE CHUTNEY

SPRINKLE THIS CHUTNEY OVER SLICED APPLES OR OTHER FRUITS, ADD SOME CHOPPED MINT, AND YOU'VE GOT A GREAT APPETIZER.

CHUTNEY

AVO CHUTNEY

THE AVO CHUTNEY SHOULD BE A LITTLE BIT TOO SALTY

because I combine it with many unsalted ingredients in other recipes. There should also be a strong-ending fiery bite, since this will also be toned down by other non-spiced accompaniments.

$^1/_2$ cup olive oil

2 cups avocado

1 tablespoon raw almond butter (optional)

1 teaspoon Juliano's Spice Chutney
  (for recipe see page 227)

$^1/_4$ cup Nama Shoyu
  or 1 teaspoon Celtic sea salt

2 teaspoons minced jalapeño

2 tablespoons minced garlic

2 tablespoons minced ginger

Serves 2

In a mixing bowl combine olive oil, avocado, and almond butter (optional) and mash the ingredients together with a masher or wooden spoon in a rapid circular stroke, until fluffy. Add Juliano's Spice Chutney, Nama Shoyu or Celtic sea salt, jalapeño, garlic, and ginger.

Makes about 3 cups.

Serves **2**

BUCKWHEATIES

THIS STUFF MAKES FOR

GREAT BREAKFAST CEREAL

or you can throw a handful on top of a salad,
pizza, ice cream, or anything else
for a little extra crunch.

5 cups sprouted buckwheat
 (for recipe see page 7)

Dehydrate the sprouted buckwheat on a solid dehydrator
sheet at 90°F for 3 hours or until crunchy. Buckwheaties last
indefinitely.

Makes 5 cups.

SALSA

RAW SALSA

1 1/2 cups chopped tomatoes,
  preferably cherry or heirloom
2 teaspoons fresh-squeezed lime juice
2 tablespoons minced red bell pepper
1/2 cup fresh cilantro, chopped
1/4 cup olive oil
1 teaspoon minced ginger
1 1/2 teaspoons minced garlic
1 teaspoon minced jalapeño
1/4 cup Nama Shoyu
  or 1 1/2 teaspoons Celtic sea salt
1/2 teaspoon Mexican Spice Chutney
  (for recipe see page 227)
1/4 cup sun-dried tomatoes (optional)

Place all ingredients into blender and blend until
creamy, about 1 minute. This salsa thickens in
about 2 or 3 minutes after blending.

Keeps for 3 days.

Serves 2

Makes about 2 cups.

CILANTRO SALSA

Serves 2

$^1/_2$ cup fresh cilantro, chopped
$^1/_2$ cup olive oil
2 teaspoons fresh-squeezed lime juice
$^1/_4$ cup Nama Shoyu
 or 1 $^1/_2$ teaspoons Celtic sea salt
1 teaspoon minced ginger
1 $^1/_2$ teaspoons minced garlic
1 teaspoon minced jalapeño

Place all the ingredients into blender and blend until creamy, about 30 seconds. This salsa thickens in about 2 or 3 minutes after blending.

Makes about 1 cup.

CORN SALSA

THE CORN GIVES ANYTHING A SWEET EDGE. TRY IT WRAPPED IN LETTUCE LEAVES WITH SOME MASHED UP AVO AND GRATED CARROT.

1 full recipe of Water
  (for recipe see page 224)
2 cups diced tomatoes
1 cup fresh cilantro, chopped and packed
$^2/_3$ cup chopped onion
$^1/_2$ cup chopped red bell pepper
$^1/_2$ cup corn kernels, cut from the cob
1 $^1/_2$ teaspoons minced garlic
$^1/_2$ tablespoon minced ginger
1 teaspoon minced habanero chili
$^1/_4$ cup Nama Shoyu
  or 1 teaspoon Celtic sea salt

Combine the above
ingredients in a
mixing bowl. Mix
thoroughly and serve.

Makes just over 4
cups salsa.

Serves 2

Serves 2

IT'S AN EDIBLE PARTY! MOST GOURMET SPECIALTY STORES CARRY THESE, OR PICK UP A GUIDE TO EDIBLE PLANTS AND YOU'LL PROBABLY BE ABLE TO GRAB SOME FOR FREE AROUND YOUR NEIGHBORHOOD.

$1/_4$ cup yellow calendula petals
$1/_4$ cup orange calendula petals
2 tablespoons blue corn flower (or bachelor button) petals
2 tablespoons hot pink corn flower (or bachelor button) petals
2 tablespoons light pink corn flower (or bachelor button) petals
2 tablespoons white corn flower (or bachelor button) petals
5 pansies, whole
20 violas, whole

In a bowl combine petals. Toss and sprinkle over everything you eat.

FLOWER CONFETTI MIX

AHEE

I CALL THIS CONCENTRATED GREEN STUFF "LIQUID FIRE." ON A SANDWICH IT MAKES HOT MUSTARD SEEM AS MILD AS HONEY!

1 cup ground mustard seed
1 cup horseradish root (pureed)
1 cup fresh cilantro, chopped
$^1/_4$ cup minced jalapeño
$^1/_2$ cup olive oil
1 tablespoon lime juice
$^1/_2$ cup mustard leaves
1 cup lemon juice

Blend well.

Makes about 1 cup.

Serves 2

2 medium eggplants
1 to 2 cups apple cider vinegar
1 medium red bell pepper
$1/2$ cup fresh basil, chopped
1 tablespoon minced garlic
olive oil, enough to cover

Serves 2

With a serrated or very sharp knife, slice the eggplant horizontally into very thin slices. Place the slices in a wide-mouth jar with a tight-sealing lid. Add enough apple cider vinegar to cover all the slices. Find a smaller jar with a lid (with no label or glue residue) that will fit into the mouth of the wide-mouth jar; fill it with water and seal with lid. Set the smaller jar on top of the eggplant slices (in the larger jar) to weigh them down. Allow the weighed-down eggplant to marinate in a cool dry place for 2 to 4 days. By hand, squeeze all moisture from the eggplant and clean the wide-mouth jar. Return the slices to the clean wide-mouth jar. Add red bell pepper, basil, garlic, and fresh ground black pepper to taste. Fill the jar with enough olive oil to cover all contents. Seal the jar and store in a cool place until desired ripeness. The eggplant is ready in 2 or 3 days, but for deep-cured taste wait six weeks. Cured eggplant keeps indefinitely but once the jar is opened it must be refrigerated.

Makes about 3 cups.

THIS ADDS ITALIAN FLARE TO ANY DISH AND IS USED IN MOST OF MY ITALIAN RECIPES.

CURED EGGPLANT

EGGPL

THEY'RE GREAT ON ALMOST ANYTHING: falafels, pasta, salad, soup, and basically every recipe other than sweet fruit dishes and desserts.

1 large onion, thinly sliced into ringlets
$2/3$ cup Nama Shoyu
$1/4$ cup olive oil

In a mixing bowl combine onion ringlets, olive oil, and Nama Shoyu. Allow onions to marinate; onions can be used after 10 minutes and can be made up to 8 hours in advance. Discard marinade.

Makes about 1 cup.

Serves 2

MARINATED ONION RINGLETS

MARINATED PORTOBELLO

Serves 2

2 cups diced portobello mushrooms
1 cup Nama Shoyu
$1/4$ cup olive oil

In a bowl soak mushrooms in Nama Shoyu and olive oil for at least 10 minutes, up to 6 hours. Note: if you don't have Nama Shoyu, substitute $1/4$ cup miso and $1 1/2$ cups fresh-squeezed orange juice. Discard marinade.

Makes 2 cups.

MARINATED

Serves **2**

PICKLED GINGER

1 cup ginger, shaved with a vegetable peeler
1 ¹/₂ cups apple cider vinegar

Place ginger in apple cider in a jar with a tight-sealing lid.
Soak for 1 minute to 1 year. Refrigerate. Keeps indefinitely.

Makes 1 cup pickled ginger.

IT'S HOT PINK AND LOOKS AMAZING ON FOOD.

1 32-ounce jar of unpasteurized (raw), shredded white sauerkraut
 (I use Fermentations Raw Sauer Kraut; it's the best in the world!)
1 head of purple cabbage, cut into quarters and sliced $1/4$ inch thick

In a big glass jar mix well (by hand) the sauerkraut and purple cabbage. Cover and set aside. Stick your hand into the jar once a day for two days and mix it up, then refrigerate. Lasts indefinitely.

Makes about $1/2$ gallon.

MELLOWKRAUT

AS LONG AS THEY'RE GOOD QUALITY, store-bought sun-dried tomatoes are just as good as homemade. But if you do make your own, use your favorite tomato. I always go for cherry tomatoes when they're in season.

Makes 1 cup

1 tablespoon olive oil
2 teaspoons minced garlic
1 teaspoon Celtic sea salt
2 medium-size tomatoes, sliced or 2 cups cherry tomatoes, halved

OPTIONAL:
olive oil, enough to fill the tomatoes' container
2 teaspoons garlic
2 teaspoons fresh oregano, chopped
2 teaspoons fresh rosemary, chopped
2 teaspoons fresh basil, chopped
2 teaspoons fresh tarragon, chopped
1 teaspoon Celtic sea salt

SUN-DRIED TOMATOES

In a mixing bowl, whisk olive oil, garlic, and Nama Shoyu or Celtic sea salt. Toss in the tomatoes and allow them to marinate for 15 minutes to overnight. After marinating, take the tomatoes out of the marinade and lay them on solid dehydrator sheets and dehydrate at 100°F until they're dry and chewy, about 18 hours. They shouldn't be dehydrated until they're "petrified," like wood; just barely dried through.

You can store the tomatoes dried and briefly run them under warm water before you use them or you can pack them in herbed olive oil. Should you choose to pack them, in a glass jar with a lid, combine the tomatoes with olive oil, garlic, oregano, rosemary, basil, tarragon and salt. Covered properly, dry or olive-oil-packed Sun-dried Tomatoes keep indefinitely in the refrigerator.

Makes $1^1/_2$ cups

KETCHUP

1 cup fresh tomatoes, chopped
1 cup sun-dried tomatoes
1 tablespoon minced garlic
2 tablespoons ginger
$^1/_4$ cup onion, chopped
8 fresh basil leaves
6 Medjool dates, pitted
$^1/_4$ cup maple syrup
$^1/_4$ cup olive oil
1 tablespoon Nama Shoyu
  or 1 teaspoon Celtic sea salt

Throw all the ingredients into a blender
(use a blending jar if you have one) and
puree. Lasts 2 weeks when refrigerated.

M AY

Makes **1** cup

1 cup RAW Restaurant's House Dressing (see
  recipe on page 212)
olive oil to taste

In a mixing bowl, whisk House Dressing with
a dash of olive oil until it has a Mayo-like
texture. Keeps for 1 week when refrigerated.

MAYO #1

MAYO #2 Makes **2** $1/4$ cups

**WHILE MAYO #1 IS RATHER INTENSE, THIS
ONE IS MELLOWER AND CREAMIER, AND
MORE SIMILAR TO REAL MAYONNAISE.**

$1/4$ cup lemon juice
2 cups cashews
3 stalks celery
$1/2$ cup chopped bell pepper
$1/4$ cup chopped onion
2 tablespoons fresh parsley, minced
2 tablespoons fresh thyme, minced
$1/4$ cup chopped tomato
1 tablespoon minced garlic

Combine the above ingredients in a blender and blend
until creamy. Keeps for 3 days in the refrigerator.

THE RAW DAIRY

12

Makes 1 $^1/_2$ cups

THIS CHEESE RESEMBLES A PÂTÉ IN TEXTURE AND CAN BE USED
AS A SAUCE OR A DRESSING IF YOU BLEND IT WITH A LITTLE
ORANGE JUICE.

ALMOND FLOWER CHEESE

$^1/_2$ cup sunflower seeds
1 cup raw almonds
2 cups Rejuvelac
  (for recipe see page 194), seaweed water,
  fresh-squeezed orange juice, or filtered water
1 teaspoon white miso
1 teaspoon fresh thyme, chopped
1 teaspoon fresh oregano, chopped
1 tablespoon chopped garlic
1 cup chopped onion
$^1/_2$ teaspoon coriander
1 tablespoon fresh parsley, firmly packed

Grind nuts and seeds in a food processor or coffee
grinder until powdery fine. Place in a blender.
Add 1 cup of liquid to the nut powder and blend.
Add the remaining cup of liquid, white miso,
thyme, oregano, garlic, onion, coriander, and parsley and blend well. You now have what I call organic seed yogurt. Place the yogurt into a jar, cover
with a hemp or cotton cheesecloth, and allow it to
ferment for 1 to 3 hours.

To firm the cheese place the jar, upside down, in
the refrigerator with a bowl on the next shelf
down to catch the whey. (Save the whey and use it
next time you're making a sauce; it gives sauces
zing.) Keeps 3 days when refrigerated.

NUT MILK

Makes 2 cups

1 cup of your favorite raw nuts (almond, walnut, cashew,
    Brazil nuts, macadamia nuts, or pine nuts, etc.)
filtered water for soaking nuts
3 cups filtered water or fresh-squeezed orange juice
a few drops of almond or vanilla extract, optional
about a teaspoon maple syrup, optional

Put nuts in a container filled with water and let them
soak for at least 2 hours. Drain nuts and in a blender
combine nuts, water, and, if desired, optional
ingredients. Blend until creamy, about 2 minutes,
and chill. Strain the milk or drink it thick. When refrigerated nut milk keeps for 2 days.

Makes about 2 cups.

BUTTER

Makes 3 cups

3 cups olive oil
1 tablespoon Celtic sea salt

Combine olive oil and salt. Pour
into an ice cube tray and freeze.
Remove a piece at a time as needed.

Makes **3** cups

NUT BUTTER

2 cups of your favorite raw nuts
$^1/_2$ cup fresh-squeezed orange
  juice, coconut water, or fresh
  pressed apple juice

Grind nuts into powder in a food
processor; add liquid. Use liquid
as sparingly as possible. Lasts in
the refrigerator for a few days.

To make the ultimate Whipped Cream I like walnuts and/or cashews best. You can use any type of nuts, but they must be raw.

1 ¹/₂ cups raw walnuts, cashews, or nuts of your choice
filtered water for soaking nuts
¹/₂ cup fresh-squeezed orange juice
2 tablespoons dates
a few drops of almond extract, optional

Put nuts in a container filled with enough water to cover and let them soak for at least 2 hours. Drain nuts and in a blender combine with orange juice, dates, and, if you wish, a few drops of almond extract. Blend, and using a rubber scraper, scrape the sides to help the cream turn over. Stop and check for sweetness and consistency; add more water if the cream is still too stiff. Continue blending until fluffy and smooth. Use immediately.

WHIPPED CREAM

Makes 2 cups

Makes **3** cups

MAC CREAM

1 cup raw macadamia nuts
1 cup raw cashews
$1/2$ cup fresh-squeezed lemon juice
$1/4$ cup Nama Shoyu or 1 $1/2$ teaspoons Celtic sea salt
1 tablespoon garlic
$1/2$ teaspoon peppercorns

Blend the above ingredients until creamy.
Keeps 2 days in the refrigerator.

A KEY INGREDIENT IN MY DELICIOUS ITALIAN PIZZA AND ALSO
AN EXCELLENT VARIATION OF ALFREDO SAUCE!

TO MAKE THIS CHEESE YOU CAN USE ANY SINGLE NUT OR A COMBINATION OF YOUR FAVORITES. I FIND SOAKED WALNUTS AND UN-SOAKED PINE NUTS MAKE THE CREAMIEST TEXTURE.

1 cup of coconut water (from 1 coconut),
 Seaweed Water, vegetable broth,
 filtered water, or fresh-squeezed orange juice
2 cups raw walnuts
1 cup raw pine nuts
filtered water for soaking nuts
$1/2$ cup fresh parsley, chopped
$1/4$ cup black miso
1 tablespoon garlic
3 tablespoons fresh-squeezed lemon juice
$1/2$ teaspoon peppercorns
1 tablespoon Nama Shoyu

Soak walnuts and pine nuts in water for 4 to 8 hours. Drain nuts and place them in a blender with the parsley, miso, garlic, lemon juice, peppercorns, and Nama Shoyu. Blend, adding only enough liquid (coconut water, Seaweed Water, vegetable broth, filtered water, or orange juice) to allow the mixture to turn over; use a rubber scraper to scrape the sides and keep the cheese turning over while blending. The cheese keeps 1 to 2 days in the refrigerator.

RAW RICOTTA CHEESE

Makes 3 cups

Makes 1 ¹/₂ cups

IT'S JAPANESE CHEESE!

2 cups water for soaking almonds
1 cup raw almonds
¹/₄ cup chopped onion
2 cups Rejuvelac (for recipe see page 194),
    coconut water, seaweed water, vegetable broth,
    fresh-squeezed orange juice or filtered water
1 tablespoon golden miso
¹/₂ tablespoon chopped garlic
1 teaspoon fresh oregano, chopped
1 teaspoon fresh thyme, chopped
1 teaspoon fresh basil, chopped
1 teaspoon fresh tarragon, minced
1 tablespoon minced ginger
1 teaspoon Umeboshi plum paste

SPROUTED ALMOND CHEESE

Fill a container with water and soak almonds for 4 to 8 hours. Drain the almonds, place them in a blender with the remaining ingredients, and blend well. Pour cheese into a jar, tightly secure with a hemp or cotton cheesecloth and allow fermentation for 1 to 3 hours.

To firm the cheese turn the jar upside down in the refrigerator with a bowl on the next shelf down to catch the whey. (Save the whey and use it next time you're making a sauce; it gives sauces a zing.) Keeps 3 days when refrigerated.

PUMPKIN SEED CHEESE

THIS PÂTÉ-LIKE CHEESE WITH A UNIQUE PUMPKIN SEED FLAVOR GOES GREAT WITH MASHED AVOCADO AND RAW OR CORN SALSA WRAPPED IN A LETTUCE LEAF.

filtered water for soaking seeds
2 cups raw pumpkin seeds
1 bunch parsley
1 tablespoon garlic, unpeeled
1 tablespoon minced ginger
1 teaspoon minced jalapeño
$^1/_4$ cup Nama Shoyu
   or 1 $^1/_2$ teaspoons Celtic sea salt
$^1/_3$ cup olive oil
$^1/_2$ cup fresh-squeezed lemon juice

In a container filled with water, soak the pumpkin seeds for at least 15 minutes. Drain the seeds and put them in a food processor (or blender) with the parsley, garlic, ginger, jalapeño, Nama Shoyu, olive oil, and lemon juice. Blend until creamy. Keeps for 2 days in the refrigerator.

DRIZZLE A LITTLE MAPLE SYRUP ON TOP OF THIS COTTAGE CHEESE FOR A QUICK ENERGY BLAST.

1 cup raw almonds
$1/2$ cup raw cashews
$1/2$ cup raw macadamia nuts
$1/2$ cup raw sunflower seeds
water for soaking nuts and seeds
1 cup Rejuvelac (for recipe see page 194),
    fresh-squeezed orange juice, coconut milk,
    seaweed water, or filtered water

Makes **2** $1/2$ cups

Put the nuts and seeds in a bowl filled with water and soak for 1 to 2 hours. Drain and place into a blender with 1 cup liquid and partially blend until the texture is chunky like cottage cheese. Place into a jar with a wide mouth, put a hemp or cotton cheesecloth over the top of the jar, and let the cheese stand for 2 hours. Refrigerate your cottage cheese. Keeps 3 days when refrigerated.

COTTAGE CHEESE

DON'T FORGET TO BUY RAW, ORGANIC NUTS NOT ROASTED, SALTED, OR SMOKED. THEY'RE BETTER FOR YOU THAN COOKED NUTS AND COOKED NUTS DO NOT HAVE THE SAME RESULTS WHEN SOAKED AND USED IN MY RECIPE

It *is* easy being cheesy.

1/4 cup flax seeds
3 cups frozen organic corn kernels
1 teaspoon Celtic sea salt
1/2 cup chopped cilantro
1 teaspoon habanero chili, chopped
1 teaspoon minced ginger
1 teaspoon minced garlic
1 teaspoon Juliano's Spice Chutney
 (for recipe see page 227)
1/2 cup fresh-squeezed orange juice
1/4 cup olive oil

Grind flax seeds in a coffee grinder. In a blender combine ground flax seeds with the remaining ingredients and blend well. Spoon the contents onto solid dehydrator sheet in thin, 4-inch circles. Dehydrate at 100°F (solid) for 5 hours or until the cheese assumes a chewy-crisp chip texture. Don't allow it to become brittle; if you do, call 'em Corn Chips. Keeps 3 days. Makes three 12″ × 12″ sheets of cheese

NACHO CHEESE

Makes three 12″ × 12″
sheets of cheese

Makes two 12″ ×12″ sheets of cheese
MOCKSARELLA CHEESE

$1/_4$ **cup flax seeds**

2 cups organic corn, cut from the cob

$1/_4$ **cup fresh basil, chopped**

2 tablespoons Nama Shoyu or 1 teaspoon Celtic sea salt

1 tablespoon minced garlic

1 tablespoon fresh-squeezed lemon juice

1 teaspoon fresh oregano, chopped

1 teaspoon fresh parsley, chopped

Grind flax seeds in a coffee grinder until powdery fine. Put powder and remaining ingredients in a blender and blend well. Pour the blender contents in thin 4-inch circles onto solid dehydrator sheets and dehydrate at 90°F for 3 to 5 hours. Keeps indefinitely.

Mo

Green Cream Cheese

AVOCADO!

Slice and spread.

GREEN CREAM CHEESE

SARELLA

1 cup raw cashews

$^1/_2$ cup raw sunflower seeds

2 cups Rejuvelac (for recipe see page 194), fresh-squeezed orange juice, coconut water, seaweed water, or filtered water

1 teaspoon white miso

2 teaspoons cinnamon

$^1/_2$ cup pitted dates

$^1/_2$ teaspoon orange rind

CASHEW FLOWER CINNAMON YOGURT

Grind nuts and seeds in a food processor or coffee grinder until powdery fine. In a blender, blend nut powder and 1 cup of the liquid. Add the remaining cup of liquid, along with the white miso, cinnamon, dates, and orange rind, and blend well. Pour the seed yogurt into a jar, tightly secure with cheesecloth and allow the yogurt to ferment for 1 to 3 hours. To firm the cheese, turn the jar upside down in the refrigerator with a bowl on the next shelf down to catch the whey. Keeps 3 days when refrigerated.

Makes 1 $^1/_2$ cups

YOGURT

Makes **1** cup

SOUR CREAM #1

1 cup avocado
$1/8$ cup fresh-squeezed lime juice

Whip the avocado and lime juice by hand or in
a food processor. Olé! Keeps 2 days.

CREAM

1 $1/2$ cups raw cashews
$3/4$ cup raw sunflower seeds
2 $1/4$ cups filtered water

Put ingredients in blender and blend well. Pour the blender contents into a glass jar and cover with a hemp or cotton cheesecloth. Allow it to stand (ferment) at room temperature for 1 to 3 hours. Taste occasionally; as soon as the cream tastes slightly sour, refrigerate it. Keeps 2 days.

SOUR CREAM #2

Makes $2 \, 1/4$ cups

GLOSSARY

ANISE HYSSOP
An anise (licorice) flavored, deep-lilac colored perennial. The flowers and foliage are edible.

ARUGULA (ah-ROO-guh-lah)
The celebrity lettuce of the '90s, this green, leafy, strong-flavored vegetable has a spicy, peppery flavor.

BEET JUICE
Juice from beets, which must be pressed through a juicer. Also available at health food stores' juice bars.

BEET PULP
Pulp of beets that is made when beet is pressed through a juicer. Also available at health food stores' juice bars.

BLACK CUMIN
A dark, rich, aromatic spice, which takes you straight to Mexico or India.

BLACK MISO
see "Miso"

BLUE GREEN ALGAE
Gathered from freshwater lakes, high in amino acids, minerals, and enzymes. Available at health food stores in powder form.

BOK CHOY
A mild Chinese cabbage with long, crunchy white stalks and tender green leaves. It resembles a bunch of wide-stalked celery with long, full leaves.

BORAGE (BOHR-ihj; BAHR-ihj)
A European herb that tastes like cucumber and has blue blossoms with hairy leaves. All parts are edible.

BRAEBURN APPLE
A crisp, firm, juicy, and tart apple from New Zealand.

BRONZE FENNEL
A perennial European herb from the carrot family, which was introduced and cultivated for its foliage and aromatic seeds.

BROWN RICE MISO
Bean paste that has less sodium than all soy misos.

BUCKWHEAT
A grain that's cultivated for the edible triangular seeds which are very high in calcium and protein.

BURDOCK
A sweet-flavored, slender root vegetable with heart-shaped leaves and purple flowers. It's a great blood purifier and is used in Japanese cuisine for flavor and good luck. Choose firm young burdock, preferably no more than 1-inch in diameter.

CAROB
A Mediterranean evergreen tree with red flowers and a carob pod. The pod's sweet pulp tastes similar to chocolate. Buy raw carob (light colored), not roasted (dark colored) carob powder.

CARROT JUICE
Juice of carrots, which must be pressed from a juicer. Also available at health food stores' juice bars.

CARROT PULP
Pulp of carrots, which is made by pressing a carrot through a juicer. Also available at health food stores' juice bars.

CASHEW BUTTER
A smooth nut butter made with cashews. Can be bought at specialty or health food stores; find the raw version.

CELTIC SEA SALT
A salt high in minerals and light gray in color because it is not refined.

CHERIMOYA
Also known as *custard apple*, it's like a mango avocado and it is my favorite food! The green fruit has a creamy, white, custard-like filling that hints of pineapple, papaya, and banana. A seasonal Central American fruit, it is now grown in California and is available from November through May. A source of niacin, iron, and vitamin C.

CHICKWEED
A herb with a slightly bitter taste. The leaves are pale green and smooth.

CHIOGGA BEET
Also called *candy cane*, this beet with concentric rings of color (red and white) is so amazing to look at that we call them "Grateful Dead-beets" at the restaurant. Use them everywhere for garnish.

CHOCOLATE MINT
A great mint variety that goes beautifully with desserts.

COCONUT MEAT
The crisp, oily flesh of a coconut, which is best accessed by using a non-flexing knife and prying between the meat and the shell.

COCONUT WATER
A wholesome, clear water found inside any coconut; crack one open and see for yourself.

CURLY CRESS
Type of green with a bitter taste.

DAIKON
From the Japanese words dai (large) and kon (root), daikon is a white or black cucumber-shaped Asian radish that's usually sweet, crisp, juicy, and white inside.

DULSE
A soft seaweed from the British Isles with a chewy texture, distinctive pungent taste, and a rich-red color. Low in calories, dulse acts like bran as a body regulator. Good source of protein, iron, and chlorophyll.

DURIAN
An enormous fruit (10 pounds at times!) of the Malaysian tree with thick spikes coating its exterior. Smells like a strong cheese and is a coveted treat among adventurous eaters. Its interior is filled with sections of creamy, vanilla-pudding-like (but way better!) fruit. Not readily available in the U.S., but you can find it fresh in some Asian markets.

ESCAROLE
A broad leafed variety of endive that is milder in flavor than either Belgian or curly endive. Available year-round.

FENNEL
A licorice or anise flavored bulbous vegetable with broad-leafed, overlapping stalks. The feathery-topped stalks are dark green and the bulb is pale green; both parts are edible.

FLAX SEED
A seed rich in calcium, iron, and niacin that's available in gourmet supermarkets.

FRISEE (free-ZAY)
A frizzy-looking lettuce with slender, curly leaves that range in color from yellow-white to yellow-green. A member of the chicory family with a slightly bitter taste.

GALANGA
A root spice and ginger relative with a musky flavor reminiscent of saffron. It comes dried whole, in slices, or in powder form. Buy only fresh galanga, which is available at Thai markets.

GINGER JUICE
Juice from fresh-pressed ginger; can only be obtained by using a juicer. Health food store juice bars can make it for you.

GOLDEN MISO (YELLOW)
see "Miso"

HABANERO CHILE
An extremely hot chile pepper, which ranges in color from light green to bright orange when ripe.

HAWAIIAN SPIRIOLINA
see "spiriolina"

HEMP OIL
Oil from hemp seeds that has a pleasant nutty flavor. It can be substituted for olive oil and is more nutritious due to its abundance of essential fatty acids. Available at health food stores.

JALAPEÑO
A small, plump Mexican hot chile pepper.

JÍCAMA (HEE-kah-mah)
A starchy tuberous root vegetable with a thin brown skin and sweet, white, crunchy flesh. Peel the thin skin before using.

KAFFIR LIME
A pear-shaped fruit grown in Southeast Asia and Hawaii that has a strong fragrance unlike any other. It is most similar to lime or lemon peel. Its bright yellow-green, bumpy and wrinkled skin and its glossy, dark leaves are used in rawing. It's easier to find dry kaffir lime at Asian markets; fresh kaffir lime is generally hard to find.

KAMUT (kah-MOOT)
The name kamut comes from the ancient Egyptian word for wheat. Considered by some to be the granddaddy of all grain, kamut is a high-protein wheat that has a delicious nutty flavor. Generally only available in health food stores. It can be substituted if allergic to wheat.

KELP
A generic name for any dried and ground brown seaweed.

LEMON BALM
A lemony tasting perennial with mint-like leaves.

LEMON GRASS
Looks like grass and tastes like lemon and is an important flavoring in Thai rawing. This herb has long, thin, gray-green leaves and a scallion-like base. Also called citronella and sereh.

LEMON THYME
A type of thyme with aromatic leaves, lavender flowers, and a refreshing lemon scent.

LIME LEAVES
see Kaffir lime.

MEADOW RUE
A delicious leaf.

MISO (MEE-soh)
A bean paste with a consistency similar to peanut butter. It comes in a wide variety of flavors and colors, and its attributes are determined by the amounts of soybeans, koji, and salt used in preparation, as well as the aging process. Varieties are barley miso, rice miso, soybean miso, and white, red, golden, and black miso. Frequently used in Japanese cooking and rich in B vitamins and protein. Store refrigerated in an airtight container.

MIZUNA
A baby green with a sweet flavor and a hint of spice.

NAMA SHOYU
An organic, delicious type of soy sauce.

NORI (NOH-ree)
Paper-thin sheets of dried seaweed used for sushi, which range in color from dark green to dark purple or black and has a sweet ocean taste. Avoid buying toasted nori.

PEPPERCRESS
A green, leafy lettuce with a peppery taste.

PICKLED GINGER
Sliced ginger that's been soaked in a mixture of water, rice vinegar, rice malt, and spices.

PINEAPPLE SAGE
Dark green, rough leaves with a delightfully strong pineapple fragrance. The flowers are scarlet to crimson, and can be used dried or fresh.

PORTOBELLO MUSHROOM

My favorite mushroom is an ideal substitute for meat. Mushrooms are full of oxygen and can be eaten even when very black (like truffles); people usually discard them at this point but this is actually when they have their best flavor.

QUINOA (KEN-wah or KEEN-wah)

A grain native to the high Andes. It looks like rice and often tastes like pasta. It contains more protein than any other grain, and is considered a complete protein because it contains all eight essential amino acids. It is full of potassium and phosphorus. New to Americans, this was the staple in the diets of the Incas and is presently used in many South American dishes. I toss it over salads and make tabouleh with it.

RED OAKLEAF

A type of baby lettuce.

RUTABAGA

A tan-colored mild-tasting root from the cabbage and mustard family and a native to Europe. Its roots and leaves are edible.

SALAD BURNET

Mild cucumber-flavored leaves.

SEAWEED WATER

A seaweed-flavored water. See recipe on page 224 for details.

SILVER THYME

A rock garden herb with silvery foliage.

SOCIETY GARLIC

A decorative herb with delicate leaves and pink-lavender flowers. Named so because you can enjoy the flavor of garlic without worrying about bad breath.

SPELT

An ancient cereal grain with a nutty flavor. A native to southern Europe, it has a higher protein content than wheat and can be tolerated by those with wheat allergies.

SPIRIOLINA

Blue green algae grown in fresh water. Buy it in powdered form in health food stores.

SUCANAT

A natural substitute for sugar made from evaporated sugar cane juice. Higher in nutritional value and a lower sucrose level than refined sugars.

SUMAC

A tart dried fruit, usually sold ground (purple-reddish powder, often mixed with salt) that comes from a bush that grows wild throughout the Middle East and in parts of Italy.

SUNCHOKES

A.k.a the Jerusalem artichoke. A lumpy, brown-skinned tuberous root of a sunflower variety. Many farmers consider this plant a weed. I chop them up to make great RAW Chips. The white flesh of this vegetable is nutty, sweet and crunchy and available from about October to March.

SUN-DRIED LIME

A brown spoiled-looking lime with a fragrant smell and a vibrant tart flavor. Grind it up and use it as the ultimate spice. Available at Middle Eastern grocery stores or through the mail: Foods of India, 121 Lexington Avenue, New York, NY 10016; (212)683–4419.

TAHINI

A thick paste of raw, hulled sesame seeds.

THAI CHILE

Only about 1 to 1 $\frac{1}{2}$ inches long and $\frac{1}{4}$ inch in diameter, this diminutive chile packs a fiery punch. The thin-fleshed Thai chile ranges in color from green to red when fully ripe and is a popular addition in many Southeast Asian dishes.

TOMATILLO

This fruit resembles a little green tomato in size and shape, but has a papery husk that you remove before using. The flavor hints of lemon, apple, and herbs. Available at gourmet supermarkets and Mexican grocery stores.

TURMERIC (TER-muh-rihk)

The root of a tropical plant in the ginger family. Native to the Orient, it is now also cultivated in India and the Caribbean. This spice with a bitter, pungent taste and a deep yellow-orange color is an essential flavoring spice of Indian and other cuisines. Its color is what makes curry dishes and mustard look yellow. Turmeric possesses antifungal and antibacterial properties and has also been used in helping arthritis, high cholesterol, digestion, liver protection, and obesity. In biblical times it was used to make perfume. Powdered turmeric is available in most supermarkets and should be stored in a cool, dark place for no more than six months.

UMEBOSHI PASTE

A sour-salty paste made from unripened Japanese plum that's pickled with brine and shiso leaf, which turns it a red color.

VEGETABLE BROTH

The juice that results from running vegetables through a juicer.

WAKAME SEAWEED

A dried seaweed that looks and tastes like spinach and must be soaked in water before use. High in calcium.

WHEATGRASS JUICE

Juice made from pressed wheatgrass; available at health food store juice bars.

WHITE MISO

Has a higher percentage of rice than soy. A bit lighter and sweeter in taste than red miso.

I NEVER USE CANNED INGREDIENTS; EVERYTHING IN CANS HAS BEEN COOKED TO DEATH—THAT'S WHY THEY LAST FOREVER. WHATEVER YOU DO, MAKE A POINT OF USING NOTHING BUT FRESH INGREDIENTS. ALMOST ALL CITIES HAVE SPECIALTY STORES WITH ORGANIC PRODUCE AND OTHER NATURAL NECESSITIES. ASIAN STORES ARE ALSO AN EXCELLENT SOURCE. IF YOU HAVE NO SOURCE FOR RAW, LIVING INGREDIENTS, CONTACT DIAMOND ORGANIC (800-922-2396), WHICH SHIPS EVRYTHING RANGING FROM KAMUT BERRIES TO LETTUCES, TOMATOES, AND A VAST ASSORTMENT OF FRUITS ANYWHERE IN THE UNITED STATES. MAIL-ORDER PRODUCTS ARE ALSO AVAILABLE THROUGH GOLDMINE NATURAL FOODS (800-475-FOOD), WHICH SPECIALIZES IN NATURAL ORGANIC DRIED FOODS (BEANS, RICE, SOY SAUCE, COOKWARE, ETC.), BUT DOES NOT SHIP FRESH PRODUCE.

INDEX